SURVIVAL TACTICS IN THE PARISH

SURVIVAL TACTICS IN THE PARISH

LYLE E. SCHALLER

ABINGDON • NASHVILLE

SURVIVAL TACTICS IN THE PARISH

Copyright © 1977 by Abingdon

Fourth Printing 1980

All rights reserved.
No part of this book may be reproduced in any manner whatsoever without written permission of the
publisher except brief quotations embodied in critical
articles or reviews. For information address Abingdon,
Nashville, Tennessee.

Library of Congress Cataloging in Publication Data
Schaller, Lyle E.
  Survival tactics in the parish.
  1. Pastoral   theology.   2.   Parishes.   I.   Title.
BV4011.S34   254   76-54751

ISBN 0-687-40757-5

Portions of this book are based on material which first appeared in *Church
Administration:* "Following the Long Pastorate (July, 1976) and "How Do
You Say Thank You?" (December, 1976). © Copyright 1976 The Sunday
School Board of the Southern Baptist Convention. All rights reserved.
Reprinted by permission. Grateful acknowledgment is made for their
cooperation.

MANUFACTURED BY THE PARTHENON PRESS AT
NASHVILLE, TENNESSEE, UNITED STATES OF AMERICA

To Shang

CONTENTS

INTRODUCTION

The central thesis of this book can be stated in four or five different ways. In broad, sweeping terms it fits under a simple generalization. The institutional skill the churches have developed to the highest level of competence is the ability to keep secrets. Or it can be stated in the form of a cynical question. Why should you as a pastor cut your own throat, or undercut your own ministry, when there are so many volunteers willing to do this for you?

This volume also affirms the old saying that it really is not necessary for everyone to re-invent the wheel. In pragmatic terms the thesis of this volume can be summarized in a longer categorical statement. If a minister wants to be an effective pastor in a parish setting, he or she must be able to survive the trials and tribulations of a pastorate long enough to build the relationships with people that constitute any essential part of the foundation for reinforcing and expanding the total ministry and outreach of that congregation. In conceptual terms it usually is more productive to stand back and look at the larger picture than to move from the details of a problem to a search for the scapegoat.

I hope this volume will help both the clergy and the laity avoid the temptation to engage in nonproductive scapegoating and consider the institutional factors that influence human behavior in the churches.

In several respects this volume is a sequel to *The Pastor and the People*, published in 1973, which began with the search by the pulpit committee at St. John's Church for a successor to their pastor who had recently resigned, and followed the career of the Reverend Mr. Donald Johnson as he contemplated the possibility of moving to St. John's, negotiated with the search committee, and eventually accepted the call. That volume was intended primarily to guide the search committee as the members sought a new pastor and the pastor as he talked with a pulpit nominating committee. Subsequent chapters followed the first year of Pastor Johnson's career at St. John's Church.

This volume follows the mythical Don Johnson as he completes a nine-year pastorate at St. John's Church. Both volumes are addressed to minsters and lay leaders. Both volumes represent an attempt to help pastors and lay officials learn from the experiences of others in similar situations. My goal is to provide a conceptual frame of reference that will both encourage and assist congregational leaders as they reflect on and order their experiences.

The methodology has been to present every insight, lesson, observation, comment, suggestion, recommendation, and question within a parish context. Several of the early chapters are directed primarily at the pastor and the pastor's spouse, but most of this volume discusses concerns that affect both the clergy and the laity. The last chapter is directed primarily at the lay leaders as they contemplate the future following the departure of a beloved minister. Much of the dialogue has been taken literally from actual situations in congregations representing two dozen denominational families.

The first three chapters are intended to be a part of a "continuing education" program as each pastor reflects on his or her ministerial career, on the influence of the predecessor, and on the responses of compulsive volunteers. The next two chapters are directed at a broader congregational audience and discuss two widely neglected issues—the invisible "signs" surrounding every church and the invisible reward system functioning within every congregation. The next six chapters are intended to stimulate congregational thinking about the development of lay leadership, the community image or identity of the church, the perils built into pastoral visitation, the temptation to cut back rather than to reach out, the dangers built into oversimple generalizations about youth ministries, and the pitfalls that often frustrate the goal setting process. The final four chapters again focus on the role of the pastor, this time from a joint congregational-ministerial perspective.

The writing of a book such as this one is based largely on the cooperation, courtesy, comments, criticisms, insights, ideas, and reflections of many other people. A few can be identified by name: Robert F. Berger, Gib Fjellman, Carl Frost, Merrill Geible, Fred Gotwald, Della Hauskins, Paul Heinecke, Dick Humke, Joe Kipfer, John Lover, Ross Marrs, Elvin Miller, Buck Moyer, John Mullen, David B. Reed, Rosemary E. Rogers, Bruno Schlachtenhaufen, Howard J. Zehr, and three different ministers with the unforgettable name of Don Johnson.

I also am greatly indebted to the air-traffic controllers at O'Hare who often provided an extra hour of two of undisturbed reflection and writing time while my plane was circling over northern Illinois, but who always made sure that we landed without mishap so we could live another day and continue on another journey.

I also am indebted to Helen Naumann for her artistic skill in turning an abstract idea into the cartoon that appears on page 103.

In his book *The Governance of Britain* former Prime Minister Sir Harold Wilson lists as the essential characteristics of a successful prime minister a sense of history and sleep. This volume is dedicated to one who has mastered three of the essential characteristics for survival in the parish ministry: getting plenty of sleep every day, a clear sense of self-identity, and a remarkable ability to ignore trifling diversions.

Most of all, however, I am indebted to the pastors and members of some four thousand congregations who have lived the experiences that constitute the foundation on which the contents of this book rest and who, by their faithfulness and obedience, have made me both grateful for and optimistic about Christ's holy church.

Finally, we come to the question of how this volume might be used by the pastor and the lay leaders of a congregation as they engage in the continuing process of self-evaluation. Obviously, one alternative is for each leader to read the entire volume.

Another alternative, which is followed in a growing number of congregations, its to set aside the first thirty or forty minutes of the monthly meeting of the governing body for a period of Bible study and prayer followed by discussion of a subject that is not tied specifically to any one item on the agenda, but that is part of the general context for the ministry and outreach of that congregation. One month, for example, this discussion might focus on the barriers to growth described in chapter 9. Another month, this time could be devoted to the possibility of establishing a pastoral relations committee (see chapter 13) if the congregation does not already have such a committee. The question of the identity and community image of the church (chapter 7) might be discussed at another meeting. Or it might be helpful for the pastor who arrived a year or two ago to use that time in discovering whether the leaders see him as predominantly task-oriented or predominantly person-centered (see chapter 2). It might be appropriate at another time to evaluate the congregation's goal-setting process (chapter 11) or the criteria used for awarding silver beavers (or dead rats) in that parish (see chapter 4). On a long summer evening it might be helpful to spend fifteen to thirty minutes walking around the property to discover what the "signs" (chapter 5) say to a stranger. This procedure might be more productive than simply passing the book around to be read by several individuals apart from any group discussion.

Regardless of how this volume is used, I hope it will stimulate the creative thinking of church leaders as they seek to be faithful and obedient in the responsibilities that God has given them in his church.

1

WHICH CHAPTER?

"When we get around to introductions in a few minutes, I would like each pastor to include a response to this question," urged the leader at an overnight retreat for two dozen pastors and their spouses. "This is the question. What chapter or term are you writing in this pastorate? If you moved less than three years ago, think in terms of your previous pastorate. If you are in your fourth or later year in your present pastorate, state how long you have been there and then identify the present chapter."

"What do you mean by chapter?" asked one of the ministers. "I'm afraid I don't see the point."

"That's a good question," came the response. "Let me take a minute or two to elaborate on the concept. Frequently we divide long periods of time into smaller units. For example, we frequently read about Franklin Roosevelt's first term as president of the United States, his second term, his third term, and the beginning period of his fourth term. Or if you talk to a ten-year-old boy, he is not simply in elementary school. He's in the fifth grade. Or an individual may refer to 'an earlier chapter in my life.' We're suggesting here that you think of a pastorate as a series of chapters, or terms, rather than as a bloc of so many years. I'm convinced that it can be helpful in looking at aspects of the life and career of a minister if we conceptualize a pastorate as a series of chapters, or terms. If you want to carry the analogy a little further, we might refer to a minister's entire career as a multivolume history. Perhaps volume one consists of a three-chapter, five-year pastorate; volume two includes six chapters and spans nine years; volume three might be a slender, one-chapter, two-year pastorate; while volume four might be a very fat book with eight or ten chapters covering fifteen or twenty years. Does that help?''

As he saw several heads nod affirmatively, the retreat leader continued, ''Now we're asking you, after you give your name and identify where you're from, to describe your career in terms of chapters. You may want to include the number of years covered by this volume. If you came rather recently to where you are serving now, you may prefer to describe your previous pastorate. Take your choice. Any questions?''

''Yes—why are we doing this?'' inquired one of the older ministers in the group.

''Good question!'' responded the retreat leader. ''Basically there are three reasons for adding this to the usual ritual of introductions. First, we would like to encourage everyone to think in terms of a ministerial career composed not simply of a series of pastorates in different places but of pastorates each consisting of a series of chapters or terms or episodes. Some of us are convinced that we can learn from reflecting on our experiences, and one way to facilitate that reflection and learning process is to conceptualize a pastorate in terms of a series of *different* chapters. Now we recognize that for some ministers this is a meaningless concept. When it comes around to your turn to introduce yourself, if you don't see either your present or a previous pastorate in terms of a series of two or three or four chapters, don't hesitate to 'pass.' I know this concept is not helpful to everyone. For example, if you are in your first year in your first pastorate after graduation from seminary, this concept probably won't mean a thing.

''The second reason for doing this,'' he continued, ''is that this is one means of helping us become better acquainted with everyone else here. If, for example, I identify myself as being in the third chapter of my second pastorate and you describe yourself in similar terms, that may offer a good opportunity for us to begin to share experiences when we break for lunch in an hour.

"Finally," concluded the retreat leader, "several of you are here with your spouse. If your spouse is a lay person we would like to have him or her wait until after you have introduced yourself and then he or she can continue the introductions for that household and comment on your description of the chapter and volume of your career. Frequently the spouse sees this division of a pastorate into chapters more clearly than does the minister. Sometimes a pastor can learn from his or her spouse—and that's good, so we try to encourage it! Now let's start over here with the introductions."

"I'm Larry Jackson, the minister of the Main Street United Methodist Church in Decatur. This is our seventh year in this pastorate. I'm just finishing the third chapter, and I expect to move in June, perhaps a month or two or three after completing that third chapter, but I don't think I'll be starting a fourth chapter in Decatur."

"My name is Becky Jackson, and I am married to the minister of the Main Street United Methodist Church," said the woman sitting next to Larry. She turned from the group to her husband and added, "I agree that chapter three is coming to an end. The first chapter ended at about ten o'clock one November evening in our second year in Decatur, and the next chapter ended with a sermon one Sunday morning in March in our fourth year. The third chapter probably ended last Sunday morning when Larry announced from the pulpit that we will be moving in three months. I guess we're not starting a fourth chapter; we'll spend these three months writing the epilogue for this fourth volume in Larry's career as a pastor."

"I hadn't thought of it in quite those terms," responded her husband, "but I guess you're right. You're certainly on target with your description of the ending of the first chapter and the beginning of the second one with that administrative board meeting in November of our second year! However, I would prefer to think of that sermon you referred to as beginning the third chapter, rather than as ending the second chapter."

''That's the preacher's perspective,'' explained Becky to the group. ''He thought he was challenging the congregation to begin a new chapter with a greatly expanded outreach into the community, but for many of the people that sermon marked the end not simply of a chapter but of a long and very comfortable era in which almost the entire focus of that church's ministry was on the members.''

''Maybe you're right,'' conceded her husband reluctantly, ''but I would prefer to think of it as the beginning of a new chapter, not simply as the end of an era.''

''It's all in your perspective,'' replied his wife. ''Remember last fall when our youngest child, Bob, left home to go to college. From his perspective he was beginning a new chapter in his life, but we felt his leaving marked the end of a twenty-six-year-era when we had always had at least one youngster at home.''

''I'm Laura White, the minister at Pilgrim United Church of Christ in Salem. I guess I'm just starting my second chapter there. The first chapter consisted of their getting used to the idea of having a woman minister, and that took about two years. This second chapter consists of bringing a group of younger men and women into leadership positions in the congregation. When I came, the 'young' leaders were people in their fifties and sixties. During the past two years a lot of people in their twenties and thirties have become very active in the church. Some were members but inactive, and many are new members. We're now in a changing-of-the-guard process. Much of the authority, in terms of offices and titles, has been transferred to these younger members; but the power, and especially the veto power, still is in the hands of the old-timers. I'll consider this second chapter completed when both the authority and the power are in the same hands, and I expect that'll take another two or three years.''

''I would agree completely with your analysis of your tenure,'' commented a man who appeared to be about thirty years old. ''I'm Laura's husband, and my name is Jack White.

I'm a computer programmer, but I'm still in my first chapter at Pilgrim. Everybody there knows what to expect of the minister's wife, but they're still trying to figure out the role of the minister's husband. My immediate predecessor in the parsonage at Pilgrim was the wife of a sixty-seven-year-old minister who had had over thirty years' experience as a minister's wife when they moved into that parsonage a dozen years ago. Practically everyone in that congregation knew what to expect of a minister's wife, and if they weren't sure, she helped them out. They left about four years ago, and after a long vacancy we came. The people spent the first couple of years trying to figure out how to relate to a female minister. Now that they're comfortable with that, they're trying to figure out how to relate to the minister's husband. That's why I'm still in my first chapter. They didn't get around to writing that one as soon as they did Laura's first chapter.''

"My story sounds rather dull compared to yours," observed the fifth person in the group. "My name is Frank Tower, and I'm the minister at First Baptist Church in Columbus. This is my fifth year in my second pastorate, and I'm clearly in my third term. I came to a very seriously divided congregation. About seven years ago the minister and seventy people walked out to form an independent Baptist congregation on the north side of Columbus. This aroused a variety of emotions among those who were left. Six months after my immediate predecessor arrived, he announced that he and his wife had agreed on a divorce. Some of the members thought this meant he must resign, but a majority wanted him to stay. He resigned and moved out of town, but this created a new division in the congregation. I spent my first term helping to bring the various factions back together. That took about two years. During my second term we completed an overdue renovation of the building, which, incidentally, greatly helped in cementing together what once was a badly divided congregation. Now, in my third chapter, we're trying to rebuild and expand the educational program, and

we just called an associate minister to help with that. I'm
looking forward to my fourth chapter, when we will focus on the
evangelistic outreach of the church. My wife won't arrive until
late afternoon; so there is no one here to correct or comment on
my story.''

"My name is Richard Moore, and I'm the minister at
Northminster Presbyterian Church," declared the young man
sitting next to Frank Tower. "I just graduated from seminary
last June, and this is my first year of my first pastorate; and so I
guess I'm in my first chapter of volume one. I'm delighted to
discover there will be a second chapter before too long!"

"I'm Dorothy Moore, Dick's wife, and I'm here to listen and
learn," declared the young woman sitting next to the Reverend
Richard Moore. "So far I've learned that these chapters
apparently are a lot longer than I thought they were when you
first introduced the idea. My first reaction was that Dick and I
were in our third term at Northminster, and now I hear Dick
admit we're still in the first."

"I appreciate the fact that I've had more time to think about
this than some of you have had," began the eighth member of
the group. "My name is Tom Berger, and I'm in the sixth year
and the third chapter as the pastor at Trinity Lutheran Church in
Middleburg. During the first chapter we got acquainted and built
the trust level between the pastor and the people. The second
chapter consisted of deciding to go into a building program, and
now we're in the third chapter, the actual construction of a
$225,000 addition to a seventy-year-old building. I've been
sitting here trying to figure out whether the fourth chapter will
consist of paying off the mortgage or developing the program
that we couldn't do before because of lack of space. This has
been very helpful because now I am beginning to see what I
hadn't even thought of before today. I had assumed my fourth
chapter would be devoted to program development, but now I
am beginning to realize that many of our leaders expect that in
my fourth chapter in this pastorate I will give top priority to

getting that $110,000 mortgage paid off as quickly as possible. I guess the agenda for our church council meeting next week should include a discussion on the contents of this next chapter. I think we may be able to avoid some misunderstandings if we get this on the agenda.''

"I'm Tom's wife, Cathy Berger, and I guess I see it pretty much as Tom sees it, except that I believe some of our members expect the fourth chapter will be devoted to church growth and bringing in more new members to fill up that new building—and also to help pay for it. I'm about convinced, Tom, that you should include all three alternatives for this next chapter when you put this on the agenda for next week's church council meeting. Unless there is a clearer understanding about their expectations of you, maybe the third chapter should be our last!''

"My story is both simple and complex,'' declared the next man in the group. "I'm David Allison, the minister at First Christian Church in Troy. "I'm just beginning my fourth year and, I hope, my second chapter there. The first chapter took three years and consisted of dealing with the grief, guilt, hostility, and pain over my predecessor's death. Late one Saturday night he went over to the church, which is only about five hundred feet from the parsonage, knelt in front of the communion table, and shot himself. The janitor found his body there the next morning. I followed an eight-month interim pastor, but the grief and guilt over his death has dominated my first three years there. I hope we have some things started now, so that in a couple of years we can look back and see a second chapter drawing to a close.''

"My name is Betty Allison,'' said the woman sitting next to David, "and I'm glad to be able to think there can be a second chapter. We've been living with two ghosts for over three years. This minister's wife died of cancer at age thirty-three, about three months before he shot himself. For nearly four years the only item on the agenda at First Christian Church has been grief and guilt. We have to get into the next chapter.''

"My name is Dick Lusik, and I'm the rector at Trinity Episcopal Church in Jefferson,'' said the black-haired man sitting next to Betty Allison. "This is the third volume of my career as a priest, and I guess I am at the end of chapter two and wondering it there is a chapter three for me at Trinity. I've been there almost three and a half years, and during the last few minutes I've been thinking that maybe the subconscious reason that Marty and I decided to come to this retreat is to discover if there can be a third chapter for us at Trinity.''

"I'm Marty Lusik, Dick's wife, and it has suddenly occurred to me that part of our problem is that Dick wrote a two-chapter book as a curate after graduation from seminary. Next he wrote a two-chapter volume as the rector at Calvary, and now we're at the end of the second chapter at Trinity.'' As she spoke, she turned toward her husband and asked, "Maybe, Dick, we need to learn how to write a third chapter rather than start a new volume after chapter two?''

As he sat there with his wife, Mary, Don Johnson was reviewing his whole ministerial career. After graduating from seminary in 1961 Don had accepted a call to Bethany Church, a 235-member congregation in a small rural community with 800 residents. As he reflected on that first pastorate he saw it dividing into four chapters. The first chapter consisted of learning how to be a pastor, and it had taken about a year before he began to feel comfortable in his role as the shepherd of this flock. The second chapter lasted about eight months and ended the day he gave up on his efforts to turn the two adult Sunday school classes into educational experiences. For years before Don arrived on the scene these classes had been primarily fellowship groups of adults who enjoyed being with one another, and that continued to be their primary function long after Don had moved away. The third chapter saw Don concentrating his time and energy on building the best youth program of any church in the community and ended two years later when a team of seven adults, whom Don had recruited, trained, and encouraged, accepted the basic responsibility for the two youth groups.

His last chapter there began about two years before Don left Bethany. During this period Don worked hard to expand the range of special events and experiences directing the personal and spiritual growth of people, both members and nonmembers. His goal was ten such events annually, and these included a lay witness mission; a week-long work-camp experience during the summer for a dozen high-school youths; launching the first two years of the Bethel Bible Series; turning the annual church picnic into a major celebration of the life and ministry of that congregation during the past year, including special recognition of all the older ex-leaders; initiating a New Year's Eve watch-night service; developing a Thursday Bible study/prayer/mutual support/fellowship/lunch/quilting group composed of nine older widowed women, three of whom were not members of any congregation; and establishing a weekly Saturday-morning Bible study and breakfast group for a dozen men.

In 1967 Don and Mary had moved from Bethany to Trinity Church, a hundred-year-old, 330-member congregation in a stable Iowa county-seat community with 5,000 residents. In 1973, after nearly six years and three chapters, which saw a 20 percent increase in the size of that congregation, Don and Mary responded affirmatively to the opportunity to move to St. John's Church. This was a relatively new congregation, established in 1951, that had seen a steady growth curve turn into a plateau in the mid-1960s. By 1973 the plateau appeared to have turned into a decline as the membership figure dropped from a peak of 683 to 525 and the average attendance at Sunday morning dropped by more than 10 percent.

It was clear to Don, even before he arrived on the scene, that his first term at St. John's would be spent rebuilding morale and raising the level of self-esteem among the members. This turned out to be a far more difficult task than Don had anticipated back in mid-1973, when he had agreed to move to St. John's. As he reflected on those first three years at St. John's, Don saw that he had been involved in six efforts concurrently. These included (1) getting acquainted with the congregation and building the trust level between the members and their new pastor; (2) changing the reward system at St. John's (see chapter 4); (3) helping the members recognize the "signs" that gradually had been posted around the property and replace them with more inviting signs (see chapter 5); (4) retraining the membership to think and function around ministry goals rather than survival goals (see chapter 6); (5) helping create a clearer community image of who and what St. John's was as a parish (see chapter 7); and (6), most traumatic of all, living through his ordeal with Dorothy (see chapter 3).

"Now, how do I describe this?" Don Johnson asked himself as it came his turn to introduce himself. "Do I come off sounding boastful by declaring that I have compressed six chapters into my first three or four years? Or do I simply say that my first term consisted of reversing the direction in which St. John's was going and that now I am well into my second term? Or do I try to rethink that and perhaps suggest that my first chapter was diagnosing what was happening at St. John's, and the second chapter, which is still being written, consists of acting on that diagnosis?"

By the time the introductions had been completed, most of the ministers were eager to discuss the usefulness of this concept of looking at a pastorate as a series of chapters. Out of this discussion came several pragmatic observations on the value of this concept.

How Do You Measure the Length of a Pastorate?

It was agreed this is a better means of measuring the length of a pastorate than simply describing the number of years served in that congregation. By looking at a pastorate in terms of ministry rather than the passage of time, the pastor is encouraged to think in terms of what is happening rather than how long he has been there. If the minister measures the length of a pastorate in terms of ministry, relationships, and program, he will tend to reflect this assessment in his conversations with members and thus encourage them to conceptualize the length of a pastorate in terms of relationships, events, and ministry rather than in terms of years. To a very significant degree, church members reflect the conceptual framework projected by the pastor. (All agreed that a major exception to that generalization occurs in the appointive system in The United Methodist Church, which tends to cause most bishops, district superintendents, pastors, and many of the laity to conceptualize the length of a pastorate in terms of the passage of time rather than in terms of relationships, program, and ministry.) Regardless of denominational label, however, the use of chapters, rather than years, is a good conceptual frame of reference to use as the pastor and the people reflect on their experiences together and seek to learn from them as they sort these experiences out in an orderly manner.

When Do You Move?

The use of this concept of chapters or terms, rather than years, also offers a useful approach to that question which most pastors raise occasionally: Has the time come for me to move?

In looking at the tenure of pastors, it appears that the dominant tendency is for pastors to move too frequently. Three patterns can be described that speak to this.

First, research on the length of pastorates suggests that a substantial number of pastors find themselves feeling very receptive to the idea of moving to another congregation approximately thirty-five to forty-five months after arriving in that pastorate. This often coincides with the end of the second chapter.

As he introduced himself, one of the ministers at this retreat described this pattern when he said, "I'm Dick Miller of the Oak Grove Church of the Brethren. I'm now well into my third chapter, but if you had asked me this same question a year or so ago I would have had a different response. At that time I would have told you I was just beginning my fourth year at Oak Grove and ready to move. As I reflect on it now, I realize that I had never served more than two chapters in any pastorate before this one and I didn't know there could be a third chapter. When I reached the end of my second chapter I was ready to move. Now that I am well into that third chapter, I can see the possibilities of a fourth chapter and a fifth and a sixth and a seventh. Today I am very enthusiastic about my future at Oak Grove; a year ago, all I saw ahead was a blank wall."

In simple terms, it appears that for a significant proportion of pastors there is a period of vocational depression that coincides with (a) the conclusion of the third year or the beginning of the fourth year in that pastorate, and (b) the end of the second (or sometimes the third) chapter in that pastorate. If this can be seen as part of a normal pattern and if the pastorate can be seen as a series of chapters, it may be helpful for the pastor to ask, Am I really at the end of this pastorate here, or is this merely the conclusion of one chapter or am I trying to identify the theme and outline of the next chapter?

If a pastorate can be seen as a series of several chapters, rather than measured only in years, it is easier to be open to the possibility of continuing for a third and fourth chapter rather than contemplating a fourth, fifth, and sixth year in the same place. The use of chapters, rather than years, for measuring the length of a pastorate encourages the pastor and the people both to think in terms of the potentialities of that next chapter. By contrast, the use of years for measuring the length of a pastorate tends to cause both pastor and people to think that the larger the number, the more likely it is that the time has come for a move. Unfortunately, in several denominations three and four are considered to be large numbers when measuring the years of a pastorate.

A second pattern has been widely studied and commented on by both religious researchers and by denominational executives concerned with ministerial placement.[1] While there are many exceptions to this generalization, *from the congregation's perspective* the most effective years of a pastorate *rarely begin before* the fourth or fifth or sixth or seventh, and sometimes even the eighth, year of that pastorate. When translated into terms of chapters, this suggests that from the congregation's point of view the most effective years of a pastorate rarely begin with the first or second chapter.

What does this pattern say to the question, Has the time come for me to move? In a majority of pastorates it probably means that if that question is being asked before the fourth or fifth year of that pastorate, it is premature. If that question is being asked in the third year, the response may be, Don't move, your best years here have yet to begin! If asked in the fifth or sixth year, the appropriate response may be, Why think about moving when you are just beginning your best years in this pastorate?

There are many exceptions to this generalization. Some of the exceptions are individual ministers who find it difficult or impossible to stay in one pastorate for more than two or three years. Another group of exceptions is composed of those congregations which begin planning the departure of the new preacher shortly after his or her arrival. In more general terms, however, there are three other types of exceptions.

Perhaps the most common exception is the first pastorate following graduation from theological seminary. Typically this is a two- to four-year pastorate, and many times it is an unofficial apprenticeship for the new minister. For a substantial number of seminary graduates it probably is best for all that this

---

[1]For an introduction to some of the literature in this field see Allen Nauss, "The Relation of Pastoral Mobility to Effectiveness," *Review of Religious Research,* Winter 1974, pp. 80-86.

first pastorate not be longer than three or four or five years. (The unfortunate consequence of this first exception is that literally thousands of congregations have a succession of ministers who are in their first pastorate—and after providing this apprenticeship for three or four or five ministers who are in their first pastorate, these congregations often need to benefit from the best years of a minister's tenure, rather than see each successive pastor depart just when the best years are about to begin!)

Another exception is the interim minister (see chapter 15), who often serves a very meaningful and effective pastorate for six months to two years or more following (a) the minister who served that same congregation for two or three or four decades or (b) the pastor who died a tragic death and the congregation needs time and an exceptionally able pastor to see them through an extended grief period or (c) the end of one era in a congregation's history, from which he or she serves as a transition pastor to the new era or (d) a severe internal division within a congregation that needs to be at least partially healed before a new, permanent pastor arrives on the scene.

The third exception to this generalization is more difficult to define. In simple terms, however, this exception tends to be seen when the congregation is ready to move into a new era in its life and at the same time the new pastor arrives. (Frequently it also coincides with the end of the brief pastorate of an interim minister. Sometimes the interim is an unintentional interim pastor who helped that congregation write the final pages in the last era in its history and also helped prepare them for a new era.) Thus the effective years begin with or soon after the arrival of the new pastor. The clearest illustration of this situation is the new mission where the arrival of the first pastor coincides with the beginning of the first chapter of that new congregation's history. Another example is the long established small rural congregation located in a community into which people are now beginning to move in large numbers. After decades of sharing a pastor with one or two other congregations, this congregation decides to affirm the change from rural to exurban by seeking its own full-time minister. The arrival of this new pastor coincides with the beginning of a new era for this ex-rural congregation.

The third of these three patterns of ministerial tenure that speak to the question, Is it time for me to move? and utilize the concept of looking at a pastorate in terms of chapters rather than years, can be summarized by the responses to these four questions.

The first question may be the simplest for some people to respond to and the most difficult for others: How much time has passed since you began your current chapter in this pastorate? If the response is two or three years or less, it probably is not time to move. If the reply is over three years it may be time to start thinking about either a new chapter or the possibility of being open to a move. If it has been more than five years since the current chapter began, it probably is time to think about moving. Very few chapters in an effective pastorate extend beyond three or four years.

The next question applies only to that relatively small group of unintentional interim pastors. These are the ministers who came to what each understood to be a permanent pastorate, only to find themselves in the role of the transitional pastor serving in a somewhat precarious situation following the end of a distinctive pastorate in that congregation's history (see the four examples on page 31), before the situation is ready for another permanent pastor. This transitional period between long pastorates or between eras in a congregation's history usually extends from six to twenty-four months, but occasionally it takes three or four or five years to bridge this transitional period. Usually the pastor who serves in this transitional period moves after a period of two or three or four years.

However, conceptualizing a pastorate as a series of chapters, rather than measuring it in years, opens the door to another alternative for the unintentional interim pastor. Is this situation one in which I can succeed myself? Can I be the permanent pastor here following myself as the transitional pastor? If the pastor and the members see this transitional period as chapter one of a multichapter pastorate, they may agree that the unintentional interim pastor should follow himself or herself and be the permanent pastor here.

A third approach is especially applicable to the pastor who has served this same congregation for five to ten or even fifteen years and is not sure whether the time has come to move or to stay and look forward to additional chapters in this pastorate. One procedure followed by several ministers is to gather several leaders together and review with them the several chapters that have been completed. After they have had time to reflect on this, the minister concludes the discussion with this request: "I wanted to share with you my perspective of what has happened during the years I have been here. It appears to me that I am completing another chapter in this pastorate. Has the time come for me to move, or should I look forward to writing another chapter in this volume? I am not suggesting that we should settle that question at this meeting, but let's get together in a week or two, after you have had time to reflect on our discussion here, and begin where we have left off here. I trust that each of you recognizes that we are talking about either a new chapter for me or a new pastor to succeed me. We are not talking about continuing the same old chapter for another two or three years!"

This approach requires an above-average degree of personal and professional security in the pastor, especially for those in the growing number of denominations where it is increasingly difficult to move; but it does offer several advantages. One of the major advantages of this approach is that it depersonalizes the discussion. Instead of focusing the discussion on the question "Do you like me?" the focus is on ministry and performance. A second advantage is that the issue of change is presented as the only alternative. Maintaining the status quo or perpetuating yesterday is not offered as an alternative. The time has come either to start a new chapter or to change pastors. Those are the real choices. A third advantage is the opening of the door for the pastor to "renegotiate the contract," to review and revise the congregation's expectations of the pastor, and to review and revise the pastor's expectations of the congregation. Finally, this approach offers the pastor the opportunity to discover the congregation's view of the minister's performance, of how the leaders see this pastor as the result of the passage of time, and of what the future should bring. While this approach will not produce a precise description of the congregation's view on these questions, it is more likely to coincide with contemporary reality than the pastor's attempting to guess the congregation's response to these questions.

The fourth of these questions on whether the time has come to move arises out of a combination of factors including the following circumstances: (1) the pastor is concluding another chapter in that pastorate, or he believes another chapter has been concluded; (2) the congregation is completing or has completed an era[2] in its history; and (3) the next era in the history of this congregation will place a different set of demands on the leadership, both lay and clergy, and call for a different set of gifts and skills from those of the present leaders.

This combination of circumstances raises a series of questions for the pastor: Do I possess the gifts and skills that are necessary for the next era in the life of this congregation? Can the next chapter in my pastorate here also be the first chapter in this new era for the congregation? Will I need some retraining in order to write a happy next chapter here? Or does this coming era require

---

[2]Examples of moving from one era in a congregation's history to a new era include: completion of a long period when the primary emphasis has been on real estate and finance and initiation of a new era when the primary emphasis is on ministry to people, program development, and outreach; changing from a long period of statistical decline and retrenchment to a new emphasis on outreach and church growth; or changing from a rural congregation to an ex-rural or exurban role.

new and different ministerial leadership? Rarely should a pastor attempt to respond unilaterally to this series of complex questions!

Differences in Perspective

While conceptualizing the length of a pastorate in terms of chapters rather than the passage of time has several advantages, it also has disadvantages. One of these disadvantages, for example, is that it is incompatible with those ecclesiastical systems where ministerial tenure is measured primarily by the passage of time. Another disadvantage is that it is primarily dependent on subjective criteria rather than the objective data that can be used to count the passage of the years.

The greatest disadvantage of thinking in terms of chapters, rather than years, in describing a pastorate lies in the differences in perspective. There are at least two important dimensions to this issue.

First, the congregation's perspective often does not coincide with that of the pastor. In talking with ministers about their last pastorate, I have discovered that it is rare to find one who says, "I left in the middle of what turned out to be my final chapter there." In reflecting on the past, most pastors describe their departure as coming at the end of a chapter in their pastorate, and sometimes this is also described as coinciding with the end of an era in the congregation's history.

The response of the laity contrasts very sharply with the pastor's assessment. When lay persons discuss the departure of the last pastor, the majority see that minister as having left not at the end of a chapter but rather in the middle of a chapter, or perhaps even shortly after the beginning of a new chapter. Some lay persons even express a sense of having been betrayed by the unexpected announcement that "our pastor" is leaving.

Why does this discrepancy exist?

While obviously this is a speculative issue, it may be helpful to the pastor who thinks in terms of chapters to speculate on this question. One factor may be that the lay person is looking at the length of a pastorate from a congregational perspective, and this does not always coincide with the pastoral perspective, which usually is more influenced by a stronger sense of impatience. A second reason can be found in the lay-professional gap. Regardless of the subject area, whether it be religion, medicine, law, communication, education, or government, most of the time most lay persons think in terms of relationships in general and interpersonal relationships in particular. We trust the people we know. By contrast, in every field of endeavor, the professionals tend to think in specialized, functional, performance terms.[3] Thus a pastor, who will often tend to think in functional and performance terms, will see the end of a chapter in this pastorate. By contrast, most of the church members (except those few lay leaders who also think in professional terms) perceive a continuing relationship with that pastor as a person and thus do not think in terms of events or program or chapters.

A third factor can be illustrated by looking at congregational histories. The vast majority of church histories are written from an outline that usually reflects either (a) building programs and real estate considerations, such as a move to a new location, or (b) the tenure of the succession of ministers serving that congregation, frequently with one chapter devoted to the tenure of each pastor. An obvious explanation for this pattern is that church histories are written long after most of the events have occurred and are heavily dependent for documentation on newspaper clippings, souvenir programs, dedication booklets, and other documents that emphasize such considerations as real estate, building programs, church finances, the arrival and

---

[3]For an elaboration of this concept and for other implications of this lay-professional gap, see Lyle E. Schaller, *Understanding Tomorrow* (Nashville: Abingdon, 1976), pp. 38-45.

departure of pastors, and similar events. It is much more difficult to document from church records the ministry of a congregation to people! Furthermore, since most church histories are written by lay persons it is only natural that they will emphasize the relationships of that congregation to a succession of meeting places and a succession of pastors. This suggests that while a minister may reflect on a seven-year pastorate as composed of three or four chapters, the typical member will see that period of time as one seven-year chapter in the history of that congregation.

What are the implications?

One of the most serious implications of this difference in perspective is that, while conceptualizing a pastorate as a series of chapters can be very helpful for the pastor in terms of career-planning and in reflecting on experiences, and for some of the lay leaders in congregational planning and goal-setting, the vast majority of the members will be marching to the beat of a different drummer.

A second dimension of this difference in perspective concerns the matter of ministerial placement. In both the call system and in the appointive system of ministerial placement, the primary yardstick for measuring the availability of a minister to move to a vacant pulpit is to count how many years he or she has been in the present position and to measure the size of the congregation. If a pastor has been serving the same congregation for six or seven or more years, it is widely assumed that he or she is available to move, regardless of the chapter or nearness to the end of a chapter. Likewise, if that pastor has the opportunity to move to a substantially larger congregation, regardless of his or her tenure in the present pastorate, it often is assumed that such an "opportunity" creates instant availability. Similarly, if a pastor is in the first or second or even the third year of his or her present pastorate, it often is assumed by others that that pastor is not available, although in some cases the end of a chapter for the pastor and the end of an era for that congregation came two years after this pastorate began.

Looking at a pastorate in terms of chapters may tend to cause the pastor to view the world from a different perspective than that of many other people, but ignoring the influence of one's predecessor will guarantee the creation of many more problems because of this difference in perspective!

2

WHO WAS YOUR PREDECESSOR?

"With the exception of the minister who organizes a new mission, every pastor comes into a situation in which the life of that parish and the first few years of his ministry are influenced by who his predecessor was, what his predecessor did, what his predecessor did not do, and how his predecessor carried out his ministry," declared the retreat leader as the Reverend Donald Johnson, his wife, Mary, and two dozen other pastors and their spouses began the evening session of an overnight retreat.

"Wait just a minute," interrupted one of the ministers in the group. "We're not going to spend this whole evening talking about our predecessors, are we? I operate on the premise that today is the first day of the rest of my life. I'm in my third pastorate now, and I've always gone in on the belief that we should always assume that we are starting a new pastorate with a clean slate. I have never even met any of my three predecessors, much less talked with them. Likewise I always made a point of never giving any advice to any of the ministers who have followed me where I served previously. In each of my pastorates I've tried to help the people understand that what is past is gone and should be forgotten. I've always vigorously recommended that everyone should act on the assumption that when a new minister arrives we are all starting out on a completely new journey together. Any trips any of us have taken in the past with other people are in the past and should be kept in the past!"

"Your repeated use of the word 'should' identifies the differences in our perspectives," responded the retreat leader. "I am *not* trying to suggest here this evening how the world should be and how people should act in their relationships with a recently arrived pastor. What I am trying to suggest is that from my understanding of the real world out there, this is what does happen and this is how people do behave. Whether it should be the way I describe it is a value question. I am attempting to operate on a lower level of complexity.''

As he spoke, the retreat leader turned and drew three lines on a sheet of newsprint and labeled them.

VALUES (How the world should be)
CAUSAL (Why it is that way)
DESCRIPTIVE (My [our] perception of the real world)

"You're raising a value question," he continued, pointing to the top line, "and I am trying to keep the discussion on these two lower levels of abstraction, how it is, and why it is that way. Now there is no law that says you should not raise value questions! Please feel free to do so. My point is simply that we will do better in communicating with one another when we are all on the same one of these three levels. I recognize that we will be successful in this only part of the time and that when some of us are thinking and talking on one level, others will be thinking on a different level of abstraction. Later this evening, when we discuss the various roles of the minister's spouse, I will make some statements on a descriptive level; and several of the spouses here will react negatively—some will disagree with my description of reality, while others will contend that it should not be the way some of us describe contemporary reality. Now, in simple descriptive terms, without getting into why it is that way or whether that is good or bad, let's spend a little time discussing some of the dynamics resulting from a change in pastoral leadership in a congregation."

How Old Was Your Predecessor?

Perhaps the most highly visible of these several changes frequently occurs when the new pastor is twenty or more years younger than his predecessor. What happens, for example, when a forty-year-old minister follows a sixty-five-year-old pastor who retires after serving that congregation for two decades? One answer is that the age of "our minister" has dropped by twenty-five years. Many members will assume, perhaps wrongly, that "now that we have a younger minister, we should be able to reach more youth and young adults." What else happens?

One of the more subtle products of a young minister's following a pastor twenty or thirty years older, who served that congregation for fifteen or twenty years and left when he was in his sixties, can be seen in the impact on a number of members in their fifties and early sixties. For years these people have viewed themselves as young when compared to the pastor. Suddenly they begin to see themselves as old when compared to the new minister. This feeling is reinforced when some of their children, who now are in their teens and early or mid-twenties, look puzzled when their parents refer to "our young pastor." If they see the new minister as old, what does this make their parents? Very few people enjoy feeling old, and some of them resent the person who has suddenly caused them to perceive themselves as old. How is this resentment expressed? By jokes? By staying away from church? By opposing suggestions offered by the new, "young" pastor? By hostility? By transferring their membership? By silence?

A second product of a major drop in the age of the minister following a change of pastors often takes two or three years before it becomes highly visible. Most people tend to associate with people of their own age. Thus when the sixty-five-year-old minister retired after serving this same congregation for twenty years, he left behind a core of experienced leaders, most of them in their fifties and sixties with perhaps several in their seventies and a few in their forties. Many of these people had served as leaders for ten, fifteen, or more years.

The new, forty-year-old minister arrives, and he probably will build his closest friendships with people from his generation. A growing proportion of the adult new members are in the thirty-five to forty-five age bracket. Within a few years many of the older leaders will start to be replaced by members fifteen to thirty years younger. What happens next?

A common result of this changing of the guard is the creation of the AAOEL group. This frequently is a very cohesive group of long-time friends, many of whom have gradually become less and less active in the life of that congregation. Some may drop out completely, while a few others may transfer their membership. The initials of this informal, ad hoc, unrecognized group stand for alienated, angry, older ex-leaders.

When Was Your Predecessor Born?

While they may appear at first glance to be the same, there is a vast difference between a person's age and when that person was born. With very few exceptions, everyone's age is changing daily, but with the exception of some thirty-nine-year-olds, one's date of birth remains the same. What happens, for example, when a pastor born in 1924 is followed by one born in 1950? One result is that the age of "our minister" drops by twenty-six years, and this may produce the effects described earlier. What else happens?

While it is neither automatic nor universal, a frequent result is a significant difference in the value system projected by the pastor. Many of the people born in the first three decades of this century were greatly influenced by the impact of the Great Depression. When, for example, someone proposes construction of an addition to the church building, the pastor born in the 1920s or earlier probably will have little difficulty legitimating such questions as How will we pay for it? For those tens of millions of Americans still carrying the scars of the Great Depression, this is a valid and proper question. The Depression

ethic supports the contention that survival is still the number-one
question.

By contrast, many of the people born into the post–World
War II era grew up in the midst of a different set of formative
influences. For them the number-one question is not survival but
rather identity. Who am I? That is the top-priority question.
Thus when the question of a building program comes up, they
are much more likely to legitimate the question, Why should we
build it?

The young minister born in 1950, unlike his older predecessor, is likely to be more understanding of those who place
identity questions at the top of the agenda and to have more
difficulty in being able to relate to and be supportive of those
who ask such survival questions as, How will we pay for it?

Three examples of how this change in the value system of
"our minister" influences congregational decision-making can
be seen repeatedly all across the continent. The first is the master
plan for a building program that was prepared several years ago
under the leadership of a pastor born before 1928. His younger
successor, who does not have any firsthand recollections of the
Great Depression, who has no sense of "ownership" of that
master plan, and who is more concerned with identity than with
survival, cannot see any reason for constructing the third and
final unit of that master plan. Several of the older, long-time
members still see completion of that third stage as necessary to
guarantee the survival of this congregation. The second example
is the congregation that, under a succession of senior ministers
each of whom was born before 1928, continued to report a
membership figure that retained that congregation's reputation
as the largest church of its denomination in that region of the
state. When the new and relatively young senior minister, who
values quality rather than quantity, arrived he led the effort to
clean the membership roll. Today, to the dismay of many of the
older members, this congregation no longer carries the

reputation of being the largest of its denominational family in that region of the state. The new senior minister neither knows nor cares what its relative size is when compared to other churches. A third example is the congregation that always ended the year with a healthy bank balance. For many members the most meaningful evaluation of the year could be determined by whether that balance was up or down when compared to the previous year. When the last depression-ethic pastor left, he noted with satisfaction that the financial reserves were the highest in the history of that congregation. His successor, who was born in the 1940s, introduced the concept of "grace giving," which includes (1) the concept that Christians live by faith, (2) the idea that the members give in response to how the Lord has blessed them, not in response to a church budget, and (3) the requirement that the church demonstrate that it too lives by faith—and this includes ending the year with as close to a zero balance as possible, even if doing so requires giving away all the reserves. Each of these three examples illustrates the fact that the value system of a congregation often is shaped, at least in part, by the value system of the pastor, and that his or her value system often is shaped in part by when that minister was born and the influence of his or her formative years.[1]

Another example of how the formative-years concept can be helpful applies to many of the pastors born in the 1930–1945 era who follow a minister born during the first quarter of the twentieth century. Many of these pastors are discovering they have a very important role as a "bridge," or as agents of reconciliation between the generation born in the first three decades of this century and the generations born since 1940. When this new and younger minister arrives, many of the younger generation feel that for the first time in their memory

---

[1] For a more extended discussion of the impact of the formative-years concept on the life of the church, see Lyle E. Schaller, *Hey, That's Our Church!* (Nashville: Abingdon, 1975), pp. 31-34 and 172-78.

they have a pastor who brings a perspective that enables him to relate both to them and to their parents. In recent years literally hundreds of high-school youth have identified to me a pastor born in this 1930–1945 era as "the only minister who has ever understood how I felt" or "as someone I can relate to with confidence" or "a person I can talk to and know he understands." By contrast the high-school youth of the mid-1970s have been far more restrained in their praise of ministers born in the 1945–1955 era.

Task Leader or Social Leader?

One of the basic principles of management is that every organization needs a person who is a task leader, an individual who emphasizes getting the job done, and also a social leader, a person who is oriented toward emphasizing interpersonal relationships. Most leaders are predominantly task-oriented or predominantly people-oriented. Some are predominantly one by a 70-30 margin, others may be 60-40 or 80-20. Very, very few leaders are 50 percent task-oriented and 50 percent people-oriented. You may want to substitute *pastoral type* for *social leader* as you listen in on this conversation among six people from four different congregations. As you listen in on these conversations, especially to the comments of the second member from First Church, it may help you understand why every minister needs to know whether his predecessor was predominantly task-oriented or predominantly person-centered.

"When he came here, our minister who left us recently was just what this congregation needed," remarked a member from Grace Church. "This parish was sharply split when he arrived. His primary task was to pour oil on some greatly troubled waters. By the time he left three years later he had helped this become a united fellowship. If I understand your terminology correctly he was what you describe as 85 percent social leader and 15 percent task leader."

"We had a real task leader for a pastor a few years ago, and that's exactly what we needed at the time," commented a member from Trinity Church. "Our people had been talking about building for twenty years, but nothing had happened. When this minister came, he was told repeatedly that we needed a fellowship hall and some decent classrooms. He agreed, and four years after he arrived we had completed a $110,000 addition. By the time he left two years after that our mortgage was down to less than $20,000. He stepped on a lot of toes around here, but he got the job done! I guess you would call him an 80 percent task leader and a 20 percent social leader."

"You've left out part of the story," interjected another member from Trinity. "First, Mrs. Gillingham, our church secretary, did a tremendous amount of pastoral work during those six years. She spent a lot of time counseling with people, smoothing down the feathers the pastor had ruffled, and helping people understand that that was just his style, that he really hadn't meant to offend anyone. In addition, there were at least a dozen of us lay persons who had to spend a lot of time on pastoral care. We needed that new building, and we probably never would have built it if we had had a minister who was primarily a social leader; but we paid more than $110,000 for it. That building cost us a lot in misunderstandings and hurt feelings."

"I believe this concept helps me understand something that happened at our church," commented a member from First Church.

"For twelve years we had a minister who, as I reflect on it now, was at least a 70 percent social leader and no more than a 30 percent task leader. Our church secretary, however, was about a 20 percent social leader and an 80 percent task leader. Together they made a beautiful team. Our minister always referred to the church secretary as 'Miss Efficiency' and gave her lots of credit for getting things done and for keeping everything, including him, on schedule.

"These two people illustrate your point that every organization needs both a task leader and a social leader.

"Our next pastor was one of those ministers who is about 80 percent task leader and 20 percent social leader. Now I think I can understand why the church secretary resigned less than a year after the arrival of this new minister. We had two task leaders, but no social leader!"

"You're not only explaining why our church secretary resigned," interjected a second member from First Church, "you're also helping me understand why so many of us had such great difficulty in adjusting to the new minister. For twelve years we had been trained to work with a team in which the pastor was the social leader and the church secretary was the task leader. That also meant that the lay leadership had to specialize in task-oriented roles. All of a sudden, when we changed ministers, we had to reverse this completely. The pastor is the task leader in our church now, and those of us among the laity who are in leadership positions have to shift from concentrating on task leadership to strengthening interpersonal relationships."

"Now I understand why our bishop picked the man he chose to be his administrative assistant," mused a person from Asbury United Methodist Church. "Our bishop is about 70 percent on the task-leader side of the equation, and he recognized the necessity of having a partner who is primarily a social leader. His new assistant is one of the finest person-centered, pastoral-type ministers in our conference. I suppose the contrast between the two raises the question whether we should pick a preacher who is primarily task-oriented or a minister who is primarily person-centered when we elect someone to the episcopacy."

Why should a busy pastor bother with this concept? There are at least six good reasons that this can be a useful concept for the minister who seeks to understand what is happening *and why*, who reflects on and orders his own experiences, and who wants to understand as clearly as possible the situation in which he finds himself or herself.

First, the recently arrived pastor can be a better and more effective minister if he understands himself and his own gifts and talents. How does a pastor discover whether he or she is predominantly task-oriented or predominantly person-centered? The simplest answer to that question for the married male minister is to ask his wife and children. If that is too threatening, a reasonably accurate alternative method of answering that question is to explain this concept to a dozen or so leaders in the congregation. After you are sure everyone understands the concept, give each one a ballot on which are written the terms "task leader" and "person-centered leader." Ask each one to indicate how he perceives the minister by dividing 100 percentage points between the two extremes. One essential ground rule is to prohibit the choice of marking the ballot 50-50. Experience suggests that persons choosing that alternative are seeking to avoid a difficult decision, rather than offering a thoughtful response to the question. For example, one person might mark 80 percent by one and 20 percent by the other, while someone else might perceive a 65-35 division. Next, count the ballots, noting how many allotted more than 50 percentage points to "task leader" and how many gave more than 50 percent to "person-centered leader." Usually the vast majority will be on the same side. Finally you may want to add up the points for each role to obtain a composite score.

Task Leader	%
Person-Centered Leader	%
	100%

If a dozen knowledgeable leaders are asked to respond to this question, typically nine or ten will place the pastor on the same side, one or two have a relationship with the minister that causes them to see him or her in a radically different light, and one does not understand the question.

Second, inevitably comparisons with your predecessor will be made by members who were well acquainted with your predecessor. You will be better able to understand and interpret these comparisons if you know (a) whether people perceive you as predominantly task-oriented or predominantly person-centered and (b) how they perceived your predecessor. To discover the latter, do not rely simply on the oral tradition! Use the same procedure, limiting the group to ten to twenty members who were very active leaders during your predecessor's tenure.

Third, the tendency in the call-system churches is to swing the pendulum. The predominantly task-oriented minister often is followed by a predominantly person-centered pastor, who frequently is followed by a predominantly task-oriented minister, and soon in the appointive system of ministerial placement, the general tendency is in the direction of appointing predominantly task-oriented ministers to larger churches and as senior ministers, and predominantly person-centered pastors to smaller congregations and as associate ministers. Why does this happen? Perhaps because the majority of the people responsible for making appointments are predominantly task-oriented? Perhaps because the appointment process is viewed as a functional task by the professionals charged with that responsibility? Perhaps because larger congregations often require predominantly task-oriented ministers?

What happens when the congregation you are now serving changes pastors? Does a predominantly task-oriented minister follow a predominantly person-centered pastor? Or vice versa? Does discovering that help you understand some of what you hear?

Fourth, if the pendulum swung when you arrived and you are the opposite of your predecessor, what does this say about the role of other staff members? If every congregation needs the leadership of a person-centered individual *and* the leadership of a task-oriented person, what does this say to the roles of staff members who served with your predecessor? What does this say about the role of the church secretary who was hired by your predecessor?

Fifth, what does this say about the role of the volunteer lay leadership? If your predecessor was predominantly a person-centered minister, did the lay leaders accept the responsibility for being task leaders, for getting the job done in church finances, building maintenance, Christian education, and missions? If not, who did this?

If your predecessor was predominantly a task-oriented minister, did the lay leaders accept the responsibility for much of the pastoral care? If not, who did? (For additional suggestions on the implications of a swing of the pendulum in changing pastors and in the changing role of the lay leadership see chapter 6.)

If you are of the same orientation as your predecessor, does this mean that everyone can continue in the same roles with the same basic division of responsibilities between the laity and the pastor?

Sixth, if the pendulum swung when you followed your predecessor as the pastor of this congregation, what does this say about the expectations the laity hold for the minister? What does this say about the expectations the minister has of the laity?

Is it reasonable to expect that the laity will understand the reasons behind this shift in roles? Or will some interpret this as "changing the players because now it is a different game" or because "we got a new manager?" If this does result in significant changes among the people holding leadership positions, will the members being replaced understand the basic reasons? Or will they assume the new minister simply wants to choose his or her own leaders? (If the pendulum swings when a female minister follows a male minister, will the people recognize that the resulting changes may have nothing to do with the sex of the minister?) Regardless of the gender of the pastor, a safe assumption is that many of the leaders who are being replaced will view this as some form of personal rejection!

If the change in ministers produces a change in leadership style from person-centered to task-oriented or vice versa, would it be wiser to offer a retraining program (see chapter 6)? Would this help the members understand the reasons behind the changes in the "rules" and the shift in the expectations of the role of the minister and changes this will produce for the laity?

One-handed or Two-handed?

After a coffee break the retreat leader asked the group, "Anyone here recognize the name of Hank Luisetti?" Only six hands were raised.

"Anyone recognize the importance of this basketball game?" he inquired as he wrote on the blackboard: Stanford 45, Long Island University 31. Not a single hand was raised in response to that question.

"This is a good time for you to learn some very relevant ancient history. Hank Luisetti was the man who popularized the one-hand jump shot in college basketball. Until the mid-1930s everyone knew that the best college basketball in the nation was played by the Eastern universities. When Hank Luisetti and the Stanford University team came East in late 1936 to play for the national championship, all the Eastern sportswriters knew that the right way to win basketball games was with the two-handed set shot. When Stanford whipped LIU very easily on the night of December 30, 1936, that ushered in the beginning of a new era in basketball.

"Joe Fulks, who died in early 1976, introduced the one-handed jump shot into professional basketball and was the leading pro scorer for several years after World War II.

"You can see the same pattern in baseball," continued the retreat leader. "When I was a boy everyone was taught to catch a baseball using two hands. About the only exception was the first baseman. If an outfielder tried to catch a fly ball with one hand, everybody would yell, 'Two hands for beginners!' Now we see infielders, outfielders, and even the catcher grabbing the ball with one hand.''

"What's the point?'' inquired one of the ministers impatiently. "What does this have to do with my predecessor and me?''

"We can see a parallel in the churches,'' continued the retreat leader. "For decades people were taught a 'right way' for operating the Sunday school, conducting corporate worship, financing the life and mission of the churches, carrying out the evangelistic responsibilities that are a part of the Christian faith, and organizing the fellowship dimensions of the congregations. The people were taught what they could and should expect of their minister. They were taught a right way to carry out a ministry to youth, and they were taught what was necessary and appropriate in a good reporting system, both to the denomination and to the members of the parish.

"As a result, today we have millions of adults who were taught to shoot baskets with a two-handed set shot, to catch a baseball with two hands, and to carry out the ministry and program of the worshiping congregation *this* way. This includes a substantial number of clergy.

"For the past four decades an increasing number of 'coaches' have been teaching people a different way to shoot baskets, to catch a baseball, to operate a Christian education program, to communicate to the members what is happening in the parish, and dozens of other things.''

"Are you suggesting we're doing a better job in all these areas than we were twenty or thirty years ago?'' asked one of the older women in the group.

"Now let's stop and look at your question,'' responded the retreat leader. "Remember those three lines I drew on this sheet of newsprint this afternoon. In the past several minutes I have been trying to stay on this bottom level, to describe how I perceive the real world out there. In a little while we will move up to this middle line and spend a few minutes talking about why it is that way and what that means. Your question raises a top-line issue, or a value concern. You're asking, Is this good?

"Let me offer an illustration of why I want to avoid that level of abstraction, at least for awhile. Fifty and sixty years ago a much larger proportion of the adult population never married than has been the case in recent decades. In many denominational families it was the custom of the churches to have men's classes and women's classes in the Sunday school. In those years the focus in dividing the adults into classes was largely on age and gender, and it was comparatively easy for a single adult to feel at home in one of these adult classes. Beginning in the 1930s—and the trend accelerated very rapidly following World War II—the custom of organizing Sunday school classes for married couples became very popular. In the mid-1950s, for example, a common practice was to have several couples classes for different age groups. This accommodated the women born in the 1930s very comfortably since they married at a comparatively young age and since 96 percent of them either have married or will marry at least once. In 1960, for example, only 28 percent of all women age 20 to 24 were still single. That was the lowest percentage for that age group since the Census Bureau began compiling that type of information. By 1975, however, that figure had climbed to 40 percent. We see today that the custom of having couples' classes, rather than men's classes and women's classes, has caused many single adults to stay away from the adult Sunday school or to choose to teach rather than be in a couples' class. Now, was that change good or bad?"

"Why can't the leaders in the churches see this and offer both couples' classes and also classes for single adults?" asked one of the younger pastors. "Why do we have to lock everything into an either-or situation?"

"That's a very, very important question you're raising,"

affirmed the retreat leader, "but you're changing the subject. First, you're moving the discussion to the middle level, the why-is-it-that-way level of abstraction, and second, you're raising a very basic question about more creative responses to pluralism. We'll get to that." (See chapter 10.)

"Now let's go back to your predecessor and to shooting baskets with a one-handed jump shot," continued the retreat leader as the group returned from these two rabbit-chasing expeditions. "The point I'm trying to make can be summarized in three questions. First, in terms of leadership style and an approach to the life and program of the parish, did your predecessor shoot baskets two-handed or one-handed? Second, were the people comfortable with the way he taught them to shoot baskets? Third, when you arrived, did you conclude that the people needed to be taught how to do things differently from the way your predecessor had taught?"

"If I understand the point you're making," commented one of the ministers, "you're suggesting that if we followed a pastor who practiced old-fashioned ways of doing things in the parish and if we come in with new, modern, and better ways of doing them, whether it be in Christian education or stewardship or community outreach, we had better recognize that we're asking the members to adjust to a new style of leadership. Furthermore, the more comfortable the people were with the two-handed set shot, the more difficult it will be for them to adjust to new and better methods. Is that the point?"

"That's not what I heard!" interrupted Don Johnson. "It seems to me that in your summary you're talking on all three levels of abstraction at once. What I heard was simply the idea that if we see ourselves as coaches or enablers or teachers we better be aware of the leadership style followed by the previous coach. You're not suggesting that if our approach is new and different this automatically means it is better. Every place I've ever been there always have been some people who did not accept new and different as automatically being better—and in some cases, at least, they were right!''

"I heard something quite different from what you two fellows say you heard," commented the youngest minister in the group. "I heard him say that the seminaries train us to use the one-handed jump shot and then we go out to serve small rural congregations · where everyone has been trained to use the two-handed set shot!''

Shepherd or Rancher?

In looking at the impact of a minister's leadership style on a congregation, one should take four considerations together.

First, if you arrange all the churches in American Protestantism on a continuum, or scale, according to size and if size is measured by the average attendance at worship on Sunday morning (rather than membership or Sunday school attendance), there are at least two places on this spectrum, or scale, where there are a disproportionately large number of congregations. The first bulge is those congregations averaging around thirty at worship. Nearly one out of five congregations averages between twenty and forty at worship, and the peak within that grouping is those congregations averaging thirty to thirty-five at worship. A second big bulge is the congregations that average approximately sixty to ninety at worship. One congregation out of six falls into that size group.[2]

A second consideration is the comparatively high proportion of new missions launched in the 1955–1970 era that leveled off with an average attendance at worship of approximately seventy-five rather than growing into the congregation of three or four or five times that size that was anticipated when the congregation was started.

---

[2]For a more extensive discussion of the groupings of congregations by size and other implications of this, see Schaller, *Hey, That's Our Church!*, pp. 39-50 and 181-86.

A third consideration is the growing volume of evidence, part of which goes back to the Old Testament, that suggests that the number and variety of face-to-face groups is directly related to the growth rate of congregations, to the participation rate of the members, and, perhaps most important of all, to the sense of belonging by the members. The creation of new face-to-face groups is especially important in the assimilation of new members. The congregation with the larger number of such groups tends to have a smaller proportion of inactive members than does the congregation of similar size and characteristics that has a more limited group life.

Finally, two images of the role of the pastor merit consideration. The more common image is of the shepherd who is directly concerned about and personally involved with each member of the flock. A radically different image is reflected by the comment of the senior minister of a large Presbyterian congregation in Texas. "When you're the pastor of a congregation as large as this one," he explained, "you can't be a shepherd; you have to be a rancher!"

While it is impossible to prove a direct cause-and-effect relationship, there is very persuasive evidence that suggests that: (1) the normal historical pressures on the pastor, especially in smaller congregations and in new missions, tend to cause him to accept a shepherd role; (2) if the pastor of a new mission accepts the shepherd role in the early years of the new mission, attendance probably will level off at an average of less than one hundred unless either (a) he changes his leadership role from the shepherd style, which is the appropriate style for the pastor of a new mission, to a rancher style of pastoral leadership and accepts the responsibility for making certain that additional new groups are created but does not accept the responsibility to shepherd each group (the parallel is the rancher who has many herds of cattle scattered among many fields but who delegates the responsibility for the direct care of each herd), *or* (b) he is succeeded within a couple of years after the founding of the new mission by a pastor with a rancher style of leadership; (3) the churches that continue to increase in size year after year tend to have rancher-style ministers as their pastors; (4) small congregations and many of the congregations that are declining in size tend to have shepherd-style pastors; and (5) after a congregation has experienced being served by a shepherd-style minister the members often resist, oppose, or resent a minister who seeks to function in a rancher-style role.

In simple language it appears that one reason approximately one-half of all the congregations in American Protestantism average fewer than seventy-five at the principal weekly worship service is the combination of the traditional image of the role of the pastor with the normal institutional and personal pressures that cause the minister to function as a shepherd. Or, to say it another way, the shepherd role is probably the appropriate ministerial style for the pastor of those congregations averaging less than one hundred and fifty at the principal weekly worship service (and that includes three-fourths of all Protestant congregations on the North American continent), but that pastoral role tends to inhibit the evangelistic outreach of those congregations.

This raises six questions for the pastor as he compares himself with his predecessor.

1. Was the predecessor a rancher or shepherd?
2. Was that the appropriate role for this congregation at that time?
3. What is my style—rancher or shepherd?
4. When I replaced my predecessor, did this mean a change in the style of ministerial leadership here?
5. If it did, what are the consequences?
6. Is my leadership style appropriate for this congregation today?

What About the Grief?

The Reverend George Hayes walked into the kitchen of the parsonage and found his wife, Lois, having coffee with Margaret Fisher. George had just returned from a quick Thursday morning visit to the hospital to spend a few minutes with a critically ill member.

"Hi, Margaret," he greeted the thirty-five-year-old woman who was his wife's closest friend. "Has Lois told you the news? We made the big decision last night, and it'll be announced Sunday. We're moving in June."

It was obvious from the startled look on Margaret's face that she had not heard a word about the Hayes' impending departure. After several seconds of complete silence she blurted out, "I guess I really don't care about your moving. I've gotten used to new preachers before, but I surely hope you aren't planning to take Lois with you!"

"Now that you bring it up," replied George, half jokingly, "I guess I hadn't actually asked her directly, but I certainly intend for us to go together!"

As Margaret continued to reflect on the news, she spoke very carefully, addressing her words to her pastor. "I don't believe I can take the chance again. As you know, your predecessor's wife, Hanna Carlson, and I were very close friends for the six years they were here. Now Lois and I have gotten to be very close, and all of a sudden you walk in and announce out of the blue that you're leaving. I don't think I can take the risk of being hurt again. Your successor's wife can look elsewhere for her friends!" With those words, Margaret stood up, announcing, "I think I'll go home now," and walked out the door.

Most congregations are far more skillful in welcoming a new minister than in handling the grief that is an inherent part of this process of separation when a pastorate comes to a conclusion. While it is true that in many congregations there are some members who are delighted, rather than grief-stricken, when they hear the minister is about to depart, usually these are a small minority of the total membership—and in several congregations they are the same individuals who are happy to see each successive pastorate come to an end. With *every* pastorate, however, there are always some members who feel a deep sense of grief and loss when their minister leaves.

In looking at this subject it should be noted there are many different people who feel a sense of loss when a minister leaves. This list includes the minister; the minister's spouse; the minister's children; the leaders in the congregation who have leaned very heavily on the minister for leadership and guidance; those families who have developed a very close relationship with *this* minister because of a family crisis, a death, or some other need requiring intimate pastoral care; those young persons who moved from childhood to young adulthood while this minister was here and who feel that this minister is the first and only pastor they have ever known; the personal friends, both members *and nonmembers,* of the minister's family; and (frequently overlooked) one or two or three other ministers in the community who feel both a personal and a professional loss as this colleague moves away.

It is highly unlikely that this grief of leaving will be dealt with adequately unless (a) the fact of the existence of this grief is recognized and accepted as normal and (b) the list of those who feel this sense of grief is recognized as a long list of many different names.

In a few cases the regional judicatory of the denomination is beginning to recognize and respond in a creative manner to the fact that the departure of the minister is a serious grief-producing experience for many people.

As the recently arrived minister looks at the situation into which he/she has just moved, there are at least three questions that should be asked concerning the grief resulting from the predecessor's departure. In general terms these questions apply if the predecessor has been gone less than three years, and they almost always apply if that time period is less than twelve months.

1. How much time has elapsed since my predecessor's departure? This may be a more complex question than first appears. Frequently the pulpit is "vacant" for several months after the departure of a pastor. For purposes of responding to the resulting grief, the *safe* way to measure this time is *not* since the physical departure of the predecessor but rather from the date I moved into the parsonage and/or I began to occupy this pulpit every Sunday. For some members the fact of a beloved minister's departure does not become real until the successor is living in that parsonage and/or is in the chancel every Sunday. If this time period is less than twelve months the safe assumption is that grief over the departure of the predecessor is still a major factor in the life of that parish and that many members are still in the process of changing their perception of the recently arrived minister from intruder to pastor.

2. Are there any special circumstances that make the grief process an especially significant factor here? If the predecessor served that congregation for more than ten to fifteen years, it may require the passage of (a) three to five years and/or (b) one or more successors before the grief has diminished to the point that it no longer is a significant factor in the relationships between pastor and people.

If the predecessor died at a comparatively young age, died a tragic or slow death, or departed in circumstances that caused the congregation to feel unusually guilty about the departure, it may be that the grief, guilt, hostility, and pain of the members will dominate the agenda for the first two or three years of the successor's tenure and occasionally for his or her entire tenure.

A more subtle factor, which often is not perceived clearly, concerns the teen-age children of the predecessor. A widely followed piece of conventional wisdom is expressed in the statement: "We can't move until a year from next summer. Our daughter is a junior in high school, and it is very important that we stay here until she finishes high school. She wants to graduate with her friends.''

What is overlooked in this statement is the fact of the tradeoffs that are a part of every decision. The tradeoff here is (1) to enable that daughter to graduate from high school with her *longtime* friends (if the parents moved while she was a junior she would still graduate with her friends, only they would be *new* friends she had not even met when the decision to move or not to move was made) versus (2) to wait to move until after the daughter graduates from high school, which means she may never again have a real "home" to return to during college holidays, vacations from work, or other normal homecoming times.

This point can be illustrated by the ministerial couple who waited until after their daughter had graduated from high school and then in August moved from Iowa to Illinois. Following high-school graduation the daughter enrolled in college in Ohio. Now during Thanksgiving, Christmas, and spring vacations from college, she stops in and spends one night with her parents in Illinois on her trips between college in Ohio and "home" (with all her old high-school friends) in Iowa. She contends she does not have any friends, except her parents, to visit in Illinois. Every time she appears in the church in Iowa she also reopens the grief many members felt over the departure of her father.

Another example of a special circumstance that enhanced the meaning of the grief over the departure of a minister can be illustrated by a church in Arkansas. This long-established congregation relocated after eighty years in a near-downtown location. The members had talked about the desirability of relocation for many years, but nothing happened until a very able and highly task-oriented clergyman came to be their pastor in 1964. By late 1967 a decision to relocate had been made, and the land for a new meeting place was purchased in early 1968. The new building was completed and ready for occupancy in May 1970. For reasons unrelated to this account the minister left two months before the congregation moved into the new structure. His successor had had a moderately unhappy pastorate and had left after three years, in mid-1973. The present minister is enjoying a very happy and effective ministry there. Recently he was asked, "What has been the most important act of your ministry here thus far?" Without a minute's hesitation he replied, "Soon after I arrived I began to realize this congregation was still grieving over the departure of the minister who led them into the relocation. About six months later, while we were discussing the annual celebration of the original founding of this congregation, I suggested we invite this minister to come back and preach on our anniversary Sunday. That Sunday that he was here I discovered for the first time that he had never had the opportunity to preach from the pulpit in this new church. Many of the members were very grateful for the leadership he gave, which turned their dream of relocation into this reality. He moved, however, before they came to this location, and many felt guilty that he had never had the chance to preach from the pulpit in the church he had helped build. Once that was behind us, the people here were ready to take on tomorrow. They couldn't do it, however, until they were past their guilt caused by the fact this minister had never had a chance to occupy this pulpit. I'm sure they saw my immediate predecessor as a trespasser, an intruder, and a symbol of their guilt for the whole three years he was here."

3. Have the necessary symbolic ceremonies that help assuage the grief been carried out? In the illustration above, concerning the minister who had helped carry out the relocation effort, this meant that he had to preach from that new pulpit in that new building.

In a South Carolina congregation the departing minister announced that he did not want any kind of farewell party, gift, or other ceremony. He had enjoyed his seven years as the pastor of that congregation, and the greatest gift they could offer him on his departure, he announced, would be to give his successor the same kind of love, loyalty, and support they had given him. Since he had been a very effective and widely appreciated pastor, this was a completely unrealistic request and placed his successor under a severe handicap. About a year and a half later a substitute ceremony occurred when three dozen members attended the graduation program at which the departed minister received his Doctor of Ministry degree and presented him with a gift from the congregation. When that ceremony had been accomplished, the successor was able to start his second chapter as the pastor of that congregation.

If the necessary symbolic ceremonies have not been completed, this may be an essential part of the first chapter in the new minister's tenure.

Identifying Your Predecessor

"Perhaps the most subtle point that we will discuss here is identifying your predecessor," observed the retreat leader as the group moved to the next item on the agenda. As he spoke he wrote some dates on the blackboard.

1930–1937
1937–1951
1951–1952
1952–1955
1955–1967
1967–1969
1969–

"The minister who came to serve this congregation in 1969 is still there and is enjoying a very satisfying, effective, and happy pastorate. The dates I have written here identify the tenure of each of the ministers who has served that congregation since 1930. The first of those represented on this list was the minister who arrived shortly after this congregation and two of its neighbors began major building programs. All three were in the very early stages of construction when the Great Depression hit. The other two met in their church basements until the late 1940s, when they were able to complete the building that was started in 1929. This congregation has fond recollections of the minister who served there in the 1930–1937 era, and the oral tradition gives him the credit for the fact that they were able to complete construction of their new building in 1932.

"Now," continued the retreat leader, "for the time period beginning with 1930, how many predecessors does the present minister have behind him?"

"Six," responded several in the group, while a couple said "Five," and one voice offered a hesitant "Three?"

"In this particular situation three is the correct answer," declared the retreat leader. "Despite the fact that only a small proportion of today's members have firsthand recollections of the minister who served that congregation in the 1930–1937 period, the legends of his leadership, plus the fact that the new fellowship hall is named for him, make him a very prominent predecessor yet today. The second is the minister who served in the 1937–1951 era. While he was there they finally burned the mortgage, and many of today's leaders joined in the years immediately after World War II. The third predecessor is the minister who served from 1955 to 1967. The other three either have been or are in the process of being forgotten."

"That's pretty hard to believe," objected an older minister in the group who had served only one pastorate that exceeded three years in length. "I can understand how some of the newer members don't remember those two ministers who were there in the early fifties; that's a long time ago. But I can't believe they're completely forgotten! And what about that minister who was there from 1967 to 1969. Don't tell me everyone's forgotten him!"

"No, they haven't completely forgotten the minister who was there for slightly over two years in the late 1960s," replied the retreat leader, "but they're working on it! The interesting dimension of this illustration is that many of the older persons who were adult members in the 1940s have completely erased those two short pastorates of the early 1950s from their memory tapes. For example, I was talking with one man who has been an active leader in that congregation since the World War II years. He had just retired from his job when I met him and was mentally sharp and in excellent physical shape. As I tried to reconstruct the history of that congregation with his help, he insisted that the minister who served from 1937 to 1951 was followed immediately by the man who had served from 1955 to 1967. When I insisted there were two ministers there between these two, he very curtly told me I was completely wrong.

"The next longtime member I interviewed also was certain there was no one between these two long pastorates. When I insisted that these two long-term pastors did not follow each other directly and offered the name of the minister who served in the 1951–52 period he finally responded, 'I vaguely recall there was a pulpit supply here after that fourteen-year pastorate, but I believe he was here for only a few weeks, perhaps a month or two to fill the pulpit.' Frankly, I believe he was trying to be polite or to avoid embarrassment, but I'm sure he did not recall either of these two short-term pastorates. The 1967–69 pastorate was a very unhappy period, incidentally, and the members are in the process of trying to forget that episode."

"How would you fit my experiences into this discussion?" inquired a balding minister who appeared to be in his middle forties. "Following seminary I spent seven years as the founding pastor of a new congregation. I went from there to be the first campus minister at a state teachers' college, which suddenly grew into a state university in the early 1960s. From there I went to start another new congregation and I am finishing my ninth year there. I'm now open to moving, and so I find this discussion intellectually very interesting; but it doesn't fit any of my experiences since I've never had a predecessor."

"Every once in awhile I run into an experienced pastor who has never had a predecessor," came the response, "and obviously that has many advantages. The tradeoff comes when a minister with fifteen or twenty years of experience without a predecessor moves into a situation where the ghost of his predecessor is still dominating the scene. When you've had ten or twenty years of practice of not having to live with one, it can be somewhat disconcerting to have to follow in someone else's tracks for the first time without any practice. This may cause a pastor to begin to question his or her own competence or to consider moving after a relatively brief period of cohabitation with that first predecessor."

Where Are All the Ministers' Wives?

"The last item we have on the formal agenda for this evening," announced the retreat leader, "is a remarkable social change. Perhaps the simplest way to describe this is to use some comparative numbers. In 1940, for example, for every 100 male ministers actively serving as pastors of congregations there were approximately 90 to 95 women who occupied the role of the minister's wife. There were a few bachelor or widowed pastors, but they were very few and far between. Today, for every 100 male ministers serving as pastors of congregations, there are only 40 or 50 or 60 women who occupy the role of the minister's wife. This tremendous demographic change has disturbed many congregational leaders."

"Are you talking about the increase in the number of divorced ministers?" inquired Don Johnson with a puzzled look. "I know the number of divorced pastors has increased rapidly during the past years, but certainly not that much, has it?"

"Don't be silly," interrupted Mary Johnson. "He's not talking about divorce; he's describing the impact of women's lib! The number of women who are willing to play the stereotyped role of pastor's wife is decreasing very rapidly."

"That's exactly the point, Mary," affirmed the retreat leader. "While the number of ministers has remained about the same, there has been a very sharp decline in the number of women willing to do all that many congregations have expected of the minister's wife."

"How does that fit into this general subject about your predecessor?" inquired one of the pastors.

"There are two illustrations we can use to relate this to your predecessor," was the response. "The first can be seen if we count roles, rather than people. For example, perhaps when your predecessor moved out, four roles were vacated. One was the minister as the pastor, one was the minister as a person, one was the wife as a person, and one was the wife in the role of the pastor's wife. When you moved in, you filled the first two roles, but did your wife agree to fill both of the other two? Or had the wife of your predecessor not filled that last one? In other words, when you two arrived, did the role of the pastor's wife become vacant for the first time? Or had the congregation discovered this new world when your predecessor's wife refused to accept that role? In effect, the first time it happens the congregation's reaction tends to be that of expecting four people to arrive to fill four roles; but only three arrive, and they feel a vacancy has been created."

"Who do you see in the congregation who is most, or least, understanding of this?" asked Mrs. Dempsey, the wife of an older pastor.

"That's an interesting question because the overall pattern, with many individual exceptions, of course, is comparatively clear and consistent," responded the retreat leader. "The largest group of church members who have the greatest difficulty with this change are older male leaders. They often suggest that the current minister is seriously handicapped because his wife does not fulfill the traditional role, or they point out that the previous pastor had an important advantage over the current minister because the predecessor's wife did enjoy doing everything

anyone ever expected of a minister's wife. By contrast women
born since 1940 or 1945 often assume *and affirm* that the
minister's wife should be seen only as a person and not in the
role of the pastor's wife. Older women and younger men usually
fall somewhere in between these two extremes on that spectrum.

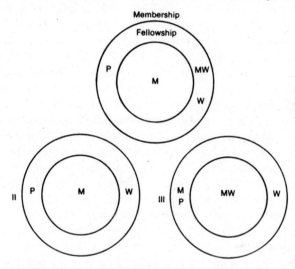

"For the second illustration of how this relates to your
predecessor," continued the retreat leader, "we have to use two
circles. The larger circle includes all the members of the
congregation. The smaller circle includes those members who
feel a part of the inner core. These are the ones who have been
admitted into the 'family,' or into the full fellowship, of the
church. The larger the congregation, the smaller the fellowship
circle in relation to the membership circle. Now in all three
pictures M represents the minister as a professional, P represents
the minister as a person, W represents the wife, and MW
represents the traditional role of the minister's wife. If the
situation with your predecessor was that shown in picture 1, that
is a relatively easy one for any minister's wife to follow. The

role of the minister's wife was relatively inconspicuous. The situation shown in picture 2 is an even easier one for any wife to follow, since that congregation has been taught to live with three roles, rather than four. Whether your wife wants to fulfill the traditional role of the minister's wife or to continue the vacancy in this role makes little difference. This is usually an easy situation for a male minister and his wife to move into, and they rarely experience any severe role problems because of the role of the predecessor's wife.

"The tough act to follow is the one shown in figure 3. Here the minister's wife is at the center of the fellowship circle, and a change of pastors probably will bring major changes of one form or another in the set of relationships between the parsonage family and the congregation. We could expand on that one in many ways, but the central point for this discussion should be clear."

As he looked at the three sketches on the newsprint, Don Johnson began mentally to draw in other possible combinations and to reflect on the implications. "Being able to picture this in my mind certainly helps me understand the dynamics accompanying a change of pastors," he thought to himself.

After the evening session was over, Mary Johnson, Beth Rawlings, and Hilda Erhart were reflecting on the discussion as they enjoyed their coffee.

"When he was describing the sharp decline in the number of women willing to fill the traditional role of the minister's wife, he really spoke to the situation Gus and I are in now," remarked Hilda. "I guess I'm the first parsonage wife in the one hundred and ten-year history of this parish who was not able and willing to try to meet every expectation the congregation had for her. Within a week after we had moved in, I had a job as a nurse in the hospital. The first two years, I was on the evening shift; so I wasn't available to play the role of the gracious hostess always delighted to have church groups meet at the parsonage. This has been quite a shock for some of our members, especially some of the older women. Although the wife of one of the previous pastors worked, she had a daytime job and apparently enjoyed entertaining in the evening and on the weekend. Just last week one of our dear members informed me very sweetly that he just realized he hadn't been in the parsonage for at least five years. Since we've been there four and a half years now, I got the point; but I simply told him it hadn't changed a bit, so he wasn't missing anything!''

"I found myself so heavily involved in each of the first two parishes Don served that I decided next time I would be more careful," commented Mary Johnson. "I taught Sunday school, played the organ, was president of our women's organization in both parishes, cooked dozens of casseroles, and worked with the youth. When Don received a teleophone call from the pulpit committee at St. John's, we sat down and talked about this. When he went for his second interview with the committee, he took along a list of twenty different items that he wanted clarified before he would consider accepting a call to St. John's. I've forgotten most of what else was on that list, but item nine was that the congregation would expect no more of the pastor's wife than would be expected of the average member.[3] After we moved, I certainly was glad Don had done this! I discovered that the previous minister's wife apparently found real satisfaction in being heavily involved in church work. She had been far more popular with the members than her husband had been, and some people claimed she worked harder in the parish than he did. I guess when Don and I moved into the parsonage at St. John's the number of minister's wives in the total population decreased by one, but Don had warned them this was going to happen.''

"I wish Gordon and I had your foresight and will power,''

---

[3] For the complete list of twenty items on Don Johnson's "negotiation list" when he was being interviewed by the pulpit nominating committee from St. John's, see Lyle E. Schaller, *The Pastor and the People* (Nashville: Abingdon, 1973), pp. 69-70.

sighed Beth Rawlings. "We joke that we took the coward's way out."

"The coward's way out? I'm afraid I've never heard of that," replied a puzzled Hilda Erhard.

"This is Gordon's third church since we were married," responded Mrs. Rawlings. "In both of the first two I tried to be a wife and a mother and also do everything that the people expected of the minister's wife. I was perpetually tired. We had three children in those eight years, and when we moved this last time Gordon and I agreed that I would concentrate on being a wife and mother and severely limit my involvement in church work. We had always planned on having three children, we had them, and we decided very firmly that I would spend more time with them and cut down on playing the role of the minister's wife."

"What happened?" inquired Mary.

"Well, to make a long story short, within a year after we had moved here I was as heavily involved in the church as ever," replied Beth with a smile. "Despite our good intentions I was again playing the role of a good minister's wife. Despite the fact that we did not plan to have more children, the next thing I knew I was pregnant with our fourth child. Ever since people discovered that we were expecting, and since Jimmy's arrival a year and a half ago, everyone has been very understanding about why they rarely see me around the church now. Gordon calls it the coward's way out!"

3

BE SURE TO THANK DOROTHY!

"I'm in need of some pastoral counseling," requested Don Johnson from the rear seat of a car carrying Don and three other ministers to an ecumenical meeting one hundred and fifty miles away. "This is my problem," he continued. "After two years at St. John's I've discovered that the hardest worker in my congregation has become my strongest opponent. As you know, St. John's was a twenty-two-year-old congregation when I arrived as the fourth pastor in its history. For the first fifteen or sixteen years it had been the typical fast-growing new suburban church, but after the second unit of their building program was finished it leveled off in growth. For the next six or seven years it drifted along with modest decreases in size and institutional strength but apparently with rather serious declines in morale, vigor, enthusiasm, unity, and loyalty. Shortly after I arrived I was delighted to discover that there was a least one loyal, hard-working, dedicated person who still had lots of enthusiasm. Her name is Dorothy Black, and . . ."

At this point Don was interrupted by a roar of laughter from Jerry, who was sitting beside him, and from the two ministers in the front seat. "We know exactly what you're talking about," explained Paul who was driving. "Bill, Jerry, and I stopped for a cup of coffee before coming by to pick you up this morning, and we discovered that each of us either had or has a woman in our congregation who is named Dorothy and who is causing us problems. We were simply laughing at the coincidence of names."

"My story is slightly different from theirs," explained Bill from the right seat. "In my case the lady under discussion is

Dottie, although her Christian name is Dorothy; and a couple of years ago she transferred her membership to another congregation."

"What happened?" inquired Don.

"Well, when I came in 1969," continued Bill, "this was a completely new congregation. I was assigned to a vacant four-acre plot of land, given a list of names, and told to go and preach up a congregation. The names had been gathered by a committee and allegedly represented a list of sixty-six persons who would be interested in being the nucleus of a new congregation. Heading the list were Dottie and her husband, Tom. It turned out that several months earlier, when she had heard of plans to start a new church out there, she had written to the denominational headquarters and offered to do anything she could to help in the formation of a new congregation. She chaired the committee that gathered that list of names of prospective members. She turned out to be a tireless volunteer. She did all my secretarial work, she organized and directed the choir, she not only typed and ran the bulletin every week, but she also gathered all the announcements for it. For the first three years, until we moved into the first unit of our building, half of our committee and board meetings were held in her home. My wife used to kid with me that if I would be willing to work as hard and as efficiently as Dottie, our congregation would pass the thousand-member mark within five years. Dottie organized the first women's group, and she got her husband, Tom, to start a Tuesday evening Bible study group that grew into a very close and cohesive fellowship with about eight of the charter members and four or five people who joined during the second or third year after our congregation was organized."

"Sounds like the kind of committed lay volunteer every minister dreams about," observed Don. "What happened next?"

"Well, as I reflect on it now, I guess she was not so much a committed volunteer as she was a compulsive worker. Dottie was a firstborn child in a family of three children, and she grew up with the strong need for the approval of others, the clear-cut task orientation, and the driving need for achievement that is so typical of firstborn children when they become adults. But while Dottie was growing up, something apparently happened that turned these natural, healthy drives into neurotic compulsions. One Sunday about three years ago, during the announcement period and the sharing of community concerns that precedes our call to worship, I forgot to thank Dottie for preparing the bulletin that Sunday. On every Sunday, from our very first worship service right up to that one day, I had always publicly thanked Dottie as well as other volunteers who had made outstanding contributions of time and effort that week. Usually Dottie was mentioned two or three times every Sunday. That Sunday, for some reason or other, I never mentioned her name even once. My wife noticed it and commented on it at lunch that day. The following Monday another woman in the congregation called and said that Dottie had asked her to prepare the bulletin for the next few weeks. I didn't think anything of it at the time; but the next thing I knew, Dottie, Tom, and two couples from that Tuesday evening Bible study group were checking at headquarters on the procedures to prefer charges against a minister in order to defrock him. It was clear that they were getting ready to prefer charges against me as a heretic."

"That's unbelievable!" commented Don. "Obviously you weren't defrocked. What happened next?"

"Well, to make a long and sordid story relatively brief," concluded Bill, "Dottie and Tom apparently didn't get any sympathy from our headquarters staff or from the people on our denominational committee on ministerial standing; so she and Tom simply disappeared, and subsequently I got a request for a letter of transfer of membership from another congregation in another denomination."

"And all this happened because one Sunday you neglected to

thank Dottie for doing the bulletin," reflected Ken. "It's a funny world!"

"That's not quite the whole story," added Bill. "This whole thing happened along about the fifth year after we had organized as a congregation. During the first few years we had grown in a consistent manner, but then we leveled off for about two years with one hundred and forty to one hundred and fifty members and about eighty-five as our average attendance at Sunday morning worship. Soon after Dottie and Tom left, the upward curve in our growth pattern picked up, and we've continued to have an increase in worship attendance and membership of nearly 15 percent a year every year since Dottie and Tom left. I can't prove a cause-and-effect relationship, but it makes me wonder whenever I hear other pastors describe how their new mission hit a plateau and didn't begin to resume the growth pattern until after a couple of the key hard-working charter members had left."

"A 15 percent annual increase means you double in size every five years," observed Jerry from beside Don. "When my Dorothy left, things got better, but not that much."

"What happened with you?" asked Don. "Fill me in on your story."

"My story parallels Bill's to a remarkable degree, except my Dorothy never tried to get me defrocked. At least, as far as I know she never did," responded Jerry. "I came to Zion Church with the clear understanding that the time had come for this ninety-year-old, seventy-member congregation to change from being a stable rural church into an exurban congregation. People were moving out there as the farms were being subdivided into two- and three-acre building lots. Zion had never had a resident, full-time pastor in its entire history. I was not only the first full-time pastor but also the last pastor for the rural chapter in its history, the only pastor during a brief transitional chapter, and the first pastor for the first chapter in its history as an exurban congregation. Soon after I arrived, a couple named George and

Dorothy Patterson moved into the community and began attending Zion. I immediately called on them, and they soon transferred their church membership from a church in another state to Zion. George is a quiet plodder but a very committed churchman. Dorothy is a firebrand. She is the original ball of fire."

"You talk as though they are still with you?" asked Don.

"Well, they are still with us, although they're no longer members at Zion," Jerry replied. "Thanks to Dorothy and some others, but especially to Dorothy for her efforts, Zion began to grow. Two years after I arrived, the membership had doubled, worship attendance was averaging between eighty and ninety, and everything was coming up roses. There was very little rivalry or jealousy between the old-timers and the newcomers. The old-timers still controlled the board, but thanks to Dorothy, who took over as Sunday school superintendent and as president of the women's organization, both of those organizations began to thrive and to provide lots of opportunities for the new people to be involved. It was obvious that we were going to outgrow that sixty-year-old frame building; so plans began to be developed to build a new church building directly across the road on a six-acre piece of land one of our longtime members, who was a farmer, offered to donate to the church. We began to plan for a building to accommodate a congregation of four hundred to five hundred members, with the potential for expansion if future growth justified it. It was about that time, for reasons that I didn't begin to understand until this morning, that Dorothy began to change from a hard-working, loyal, activist, dedicated ally to an undercover enemy."

"What happened this morning," inquired Don, "that has helped you understand this better?"

"It began with our conversation this morning and has continued with this discussion," replied Jerry. "For example, I just realized that my Dorothy was the firstborn of three children in her family and her personality conforms exactly to what Bill described a few minutes ago as typical characteristics of the firstborn child."

"What happened to her? Where did she and her husband go?" persisted Don. "You said they're still with you, but no longer members."

"Well," replied Jerry, "when we got into serious discussions on the building program it was obvious this was going to become a much larger congregation. So, toward the end of my third year at Zion, Dorothy got on the telephone and began to call her friends. Within about six months she had recruited five other families, and they all left to join a small independent church about a mile from our property."

"Why do you think she left?" persisted Don.

"Well, at first I took it personally and thought it was something I had done or not done, but this morning's discussion leads me to believe that I had very little to do with it. Dorothy needed lots of affirmation, she needed to be a big frog in a little pond, and when she saw our pond was going to grow and there might be frogs in it bigger than she, that meant she had to leave."

"Let me fill you in on my Dorothy," interrupted Paul from behind the wheel. "That may help you see the broad generalizations a little clearer."

"Aren't you going to give me a chance to tell you the rest of my story?" laughed Don. "Are you all so wrapped up in your own Dorothys that you think you can help me without even hearing my story?"

"Yes, I think we can solve your problem without hearing it," replied Bill with great confidence in his voice from the right front seat. "I think the three of us have had enough experience with Dorothys that we can give you all the advice you need without hearing any more of your story."

"My Dorothy is much like Bill's," continued Paul. "She was a charter member of a new mission I organized and served for seven years. She was a compulsive worker, a firstborn child, sweet and pleasant but authoritarian, and a tremendous help in those first four years. About the time we reached one hundred in worship attendance and were beginning plans for our second building unit, Dorothy got mad because, she said, I didn't really appreciate all she had done. Shortly thereafter, she recruited a dozen other charter members, and one Sunday they all started going to another church a couple of miles away. A few weeks later I got a letter from that minister asking for letters of transfer for fifteen of our members, including Dorothy and her husband. During the next two years our congregation grew faster than it ever has before or since.''

"So what?" inquired Don in an innocent tone of voice.

"So that explains why Paul was opposed to women speaking in church," replied Paul as he quickly darted around a slow-moving truck full of lumber. "After all, remember, he was a mission pastor out starting new congregations!"

"Well, whether you guys want to hear it or not," persisted Don, "I'm going to tell you about the Dorothy who is out to undercut my ministry at St. John's. I remember very clearly the first time I met her. It was my second week at St. John's, and we had a Christian Education Committee scheduled for 8:00 that evening. Another group had been meeting from 6:30 to 7:30, and I was sitting there by a table talking with one of the members who had to be at both meetings. When Dorothy came in I stood up and greeted her. Without stopping, she introduced herself and immediately began to gather up the dirty coffee cups and ashtrays and to clean up the place."

The Adult Who Was Firstborn

"That's Dorothy, all right," exclaimed Bill. "The woman who was the firstborn child in her family and has this compulsion to be neat, clean, and orderly."

"Now wait a minute, Bill," exclaimed Paul. "You're pushing this firstborn business a little hard here, aren't you?

After all, I was the firstborn child in our family. There's nothing wrong with being a firstborn!''

"I was the firstborn in my family," added Jerry.

"So was I," commented Don.

"That figures," observed Bill. "While slightly less than one-third of the adult population consists of firstborn children, they account for well over half of all teachers, ministers, persons in the helping professions, army officers, engineers, architects, chemists, mathematicians, and Navy pilots. Twenty-one of the first twenty-three astronauts were firstborn children. The law of averages says that in a car with four clergymen in it, two or three probably will be firstborn children." [1]

"Are we talking about the characteristics of adults who were the firstborn children in their families, about your Dorothys, or about my problem that I never have had a chance to explain to you egotistical preachers who've forgotten that neighbor-centered love is also supposed to include your fellow pastor?" asked Don with a mixture of humor and impatience in his voice.

"Your selfish need to have your problems dominate the agenda of this erudite discussion is really a sub-subsection under the overall category of 'Dorothy,' which is the major heading in this outline," responded Bill. "Your insistence on displaying your verbal skills before others, your very strong task orientation, and your tendency to be fearful in the stress-producing situation we have here in this car are simply manifestations of the characteristics of the typical firstborn child. As the third-born in a family of five, I naturally tend to be

---

[1] Anyone wishing to explore the implications of birth order further should turn to Alfred Adler, *What Life Should Mean to You* (New York: Capricorn, 1958); J. H. S. Bossard, *The Large Family System: An Original Study in the Sociology of Family Behavior* (Philadelphia: University of Pennsylvania Press, 1956); William D. Althus, "Birth Order and Its Sequence," *Science,* January, 1966, pp. 44-49; Walter Toman, *Family Constellation,* 2nd ed. (New York: Springer Publishing Co., 1969); Lucille Forer, *Birth Order and Life Roles* (Springfield, Ill.: Charles C. Thomas, 1961); Lucille Forer with Henry Still, *The Birth Order Factor* (New York: David McKay, 1976).

self-reliant, to relate well to others in situations such as this one, to perform well under stress, to have less need for approval of the group, to be eager to help and to serve others, and to be more of a social leader than a task leader. Therefore, if you'll shut up and listen, Don, we'll solve all your problems for you, and you'll learn more on this trip than you ever learned in seminary.''

"I trust you know Bill well enough by this time to know he's only kidding,'' whispered Jerry in Don's ear.

"Seriously,'' continued Bill, "I think we can say several things about your Dorothy without hearing any more from you. But we also may miss the situation completely. In our discussions earlier this morning, before we picked you up, we came to several conclusions. Let me add what has been said here, and then you tell us how irrelevant this is to your situation.

"The Dorothys we have been talking about were all firstborn children, which may or may not be very significant. I believe it is of some relevance. She tends to be a compulsive worker who has an exceptionally strong need of affirmation, she works very hard to be accepted, she soaks up expressions of gratitude like water poured on the desert sand—the more she gets the more she needs—and she tends to specialize in those tasks which give her a great deal of satisfaction because she can see immediate, tangible, and visible results of her work. Preparing the bulletin, serving on the altar guild, organizing a new group or class, cleaning up the kitchen at the church, decorating the church for a party, or putting up a display on the bulletin board are examples of this. She is less likely to be interested in the low visibility responsibilities where tangible results are less evident, such as teaching a Sunday school class of children, taking care of the church nursery, calling on the sick and shut-in, or serving on a committee.

"She tends to find fulfillment in being the hardest worker in a small congregation where everyone can see what she has done and shower her with words of gratitude. As the congregation increases in size her position becomes threatened because it is obvious that the larger the congregation, the smaller the proportion of the members who will be aware of and grateful for all she does. For example, the Dottie in my parish organized the women's group and was president of it for the first two years of its existence. I suggested that since we had over two dozen women in it, it be divided into two or three circles that would meet monthly and they could have general meetings six or eight times a year. Dottie completely and successfully resisted this suggestion. I offered it with the expectation this would provide more opportunities to involve more women and to facilitate the assimilation of new members. Many months later I discovered that she had accused me of offering this suggestion in order to destroy the women's organization. She told several women that I was completely opposed to having a separate women's organization in the church. I think the problem was that if the women's group had been divided into circles, it would have reduced her visibility and fewer people would have been dependent on her. One of the characteristics of Dorothy is she needs to feel that others are dependent on her. Wherever she goes or whatever she does, she builds and reinforces this dependency relationship.''

"That's right," agreed Paul, "and when the congregation reaches a size that it is obvious no one is indispensable, she begins to feel threatened."

"So when she begins to feel threatened because of the growing size of the congregation, she takes aim at the person she identifies as the cause of the threat, and that usually is the minister," added Jerry.

"Or if the pastor forgets to thank her publicly for what she has done as a volunteer, she may feel threatened because apparently the pastor is not affirming his dependence on her or because the congregation is growing so large the pastor no longer is fully aware of how dependent he really is on her. Thus it is impossible for the pastor to thank her too frequently or too profusely.''

"But your biggest thank-you should be reserved for when she leaves you for another congregation," interjected Paul, "because that is when she is really doing you and the congregation a big favor. By leaving she opens up the door for meaningful involvement and participation by several other people, and thus you have a broader base of ownership of what is happening in the parish. As long as Dorothy is around, by doing so many different things she freezes other people out and inhibits the chances for outreach and growth."

"Wait a minute," interjected Jerry. "Perhaps we're being a little harsh on Dorothy. I remember hearing one of our synod-staff men saying that the typical new mission usually hit a plateau in its growth curve and frequently stayed on that plateau until a half-dozen of the key charter members left and, by leaving, created some vacancies to be filled by new members. Maybe it's not all Dorothy's fault. She may have lots of help in freezing out potential new leaders."

"Now, have we helped you with your problem with your Dorothy?" asked Bill as he turned and looked over his left shoulder at Don.

"No, not much," replied Don Johnson. "My Dorothy has only a 10 or 15 percent overlap with the picture you have drawn of your Dorothys, but this surely has been helpful to me in understanding the behavior pattern of one of the men at St. John's!"

4

SILVER BEAVERS OR DEAD RATS?

The Carol Choir at Community Church had spent many Thursday afternoons after school rehearsing for their presentation of the cantata *David and the Giants*. When the Sunday morning rolled around that they were going to present it to the congregation during the worship service, the children were somewhat nervous, but it was an overwhelming success. The congregation responded with four minutes of standing applause.

Everyone agreed that the congregation had awarded the Carol Choir, its director, and the accompanist a huge "Silver Beaver" for their performance.

The Boy Scouts of America have developed three major awards for distinguished service by adults. The Silver Buffalo, first awarded in 1926, is given for distinguished service by an adult to boys on a general or national level. The Silver Beaver was first awarded in 1931 and is given for distinguished service to boys within a local council. The Silver Antelope, first awarded in 1943, is given for distinguished service by an adult within a region. From a congregational perspective, the Silver Beaver is equivalent to the thank-you given to volunteers by a congregation or a local group of churches.

Every congregation has it own form of Silver Beaver awards. Every congregation, by one means or another, hands out awards to members. These vary from a quiet thank-you to a vigorous pat on the back to the subtle deference accorded the person believed to be the largest financial contributor to a major celebration in honor of a departing minister. In other words, every congregation hands out a number of Silver Beavers every year.

In April 1974, Mrs. Robert Davis was asked to be the temporary substitute teacher for the third- and fourth-grade class at Grace Church. During the summer of 1975, after Mrs. Davis had given seventeen months of service as a temporary substitute, the Sunday school superintendent called her on the telephone and announced: "I'm sorry it has taken so long, but we've finally found a qualified teacher for the third- and fourth-grade class. The new teacher will begin a week from this coming Sunday, and I'm sure you will rejoice with the rest of us that we've finally found someone to take over that class. One more Sunday, and you can consider your obligation has come to an end."

Grace Church is more skillful in handing out dead rats than in awarding Silver Beavers to the members.

As the years passed at Bethlehem Church the members of the altar guild grew fewer in number until finally the dependable members consisted of eight women, the youngest of whom was seventy-three. The newly arrived pastor found their work to be completely unsatisfactory. Finally he took his problem to the fifty-seven-year-old president of the congregation. This very influential lay leader responded by explaining that the previous pastor had complained on the same point and since they had not been successful in recruiting any younger members for the altar guild, perhaps the best course of action would be to abolish it. The pastor agreed, with the reservation that as time passed and he became better acquainted with the congregation he would be free to organize a new altar guild. Accordingly, at its next meeting the church council adopted a resolution abolishing the altar guild, to be effective one month later.

At the same meeting the pastor suggested that since the newest member of the altar guild had served as a member of that group for twenty-two years, the church council authorize having certificates printed, one for each of the women, thanking them for their many years of faithful volunteer service. After these had been signed by the president of the congregation and the pastor, they would be framed; and during a Sunday morning worship service each of these eight longtime members would be presented with this symbol of the congregation's appreciation.

"That'll cost a chunk of money," objected one member of the church council.

"I agree," announced the man who also chaired the finance committee. "Why couldn't we simply have a personal letter typed for each of these ladies, have this signed by the president of the congregation and the pastor, and present these to them during a worship service?"

"If we start that, where do we stop?" asked another member of the church council. "Pretty soon we'll have to present a fancy certificate every time someone bakes a cake or helps clean up the church! We'll need a full-time secretary just to keep up with typing the thank-you letters."

Finally, after fifteen minutes of discussion it was agreed that the pastor would write a brief note of thanks to all the members of the altar guild and this would appear in next month's issue of the mimeographed parish newsletter.

As a result of several years of practice the church council of Bethlehem Church has developed an unusually high level of competence at turning potential Silver Beavers into dead rats.

Carla Wagner's husband died when she was thirty-four, nine years after the birth of their third child. She went back to work as a nurse; and for the next thirty years she combined her jobs as a mother, as the office nurse to the only physician in a nearby city of seventeen hundred residents, as a very active member in the one hundred thirty-member church in the small community in which she continued to live, and as the chief source of medical advice at all hours in that community of two hundred residents. When Carla retired after thirty years, several people from this small congregation formed a committee and sponsored a recognition dinner and retirement party for Carla that was attended by nearly five hundred people.

That same week Walter Smith, a seventy-four-year-old retired farmer, and his seventy-one-year-old wife, Mary, completed their twentieth year as the unpaid janitors at the white frame building housing this one hundred thirty-member congregation. No one mentioned this anniversary that week, but one member complained that he should cut the grass on Friday, rather than on Tuesday, every week so it would look better on Sunday.

The unofficial policy in this congregation is that for every Silver Beaver awarded a member, someone else receives a dead rat.

Mr. and Mrs. William A. Rogers had served for two years as co-presidents of the couples Sunday school class at Westminster Church. Their primary responsibilities had been to chair the quarterly meetings of the officers of the class, to find people to teach the class each Sunday (they usually had the same teacher for two to six consecutive Sundays), and to make sure there were ten social get-togethers of the class during the year. This class originated as the young couples class in the the post–World War II era, it dropped the word "young" from the name in the mid-1960s, and today two-thirds of the influential leaders at Westminster come from this class. When Bill and Marie Rogers completed their two-year term, the class presented them with an engraved silver tray in gratitude for their work.

That same week Mrs. Roy Gilmore completed her sixth year teaching fourth-grade Sunday school. If her husband had not taken her out to dinner in recognition of that date, it would have passed completely unnoticed.

The informal policy at Westminster Church is to give Silver Beavers to adult volunteers who work with adults and to award dead rats to people who teach in the children's department.

Not If, But How and Who

Whenever this subject is brought up at a meeting of congregational leaders, the most frequent responses include such objections as these: "But we can't do that! If we ever started that, where would we stop?" "If you start handing out awards for meritorious service in the church, you're bound to miss some deserving people and needlessly hurt their feelings." "Why should people expect a formal thank-you? After all, what they do in the life of the church is done to please God, not man. Our members don't expect any awards or thanks. They do what they do because they love the Lord and are loyal to this church." "If we got into that game, what would we use for criteria in handing out awards?"

These objections have a persuasive ring to them, but they miss the point. In one form or another *every* congregation does express its gratitude to members for what they contribute in time, energy, talents, money, and service. The question is not *whether* this happens but rather, *how* will it be done and what criteria will be used in handing out the ecclesiastical version of Scouting's Silver Beaver?

Three Questions on Criteria

The members of every congregation develop their own criteria in determining who are thanked for their efforts in the church as well as the method for expressing their gratitude. For those congregations seeking to become more intentional in this process, it may be helpful to look at three questions about criteria.

First, regardless of how informal the system may be for saying thank you to some members, it is possible to step back, look at the process, and identify the criteria being used. Are these criteria consistent with the value system of a Christian congregation? Are these criteria consistent with the goals of *this* congregation?

Second, the congregations that have been most satisfied with intentional and systematic efforts to thank deserving members have stressed faithfulness and obedience as the basic criteria in selecting people to be recognized. That is what the Lord asks of each of us, and these are better yardsticks than wealth, heritage, leadership skills, brilliance, or personality. What are the criteria used in your congregation?

Third, there appears to be a general trend in the churches to reward verbal skills rather than skills requiring the use of the hands. This can be seen in the selection of persons with a high degree of verbal skill to be congregational leaders, as well as in the elimination of many events such as church dinners, work days at the church, bazaars and handicraft exhibits, which place a premium on creative skills using the hands rather than the tongue. Do you reward verbal skills or creative skills in your congregation?

What are the methods a congregation can use in expressing its gratitude to the members in a manner that will be intentional and consistent with the value system and goals of that congregation? It may be helpful to look at three different approaches. Perhaps you can adapt one of these to your situation.

Churchman of the Week

Many congregations pick a churchman of the week or of the month. The recipient of this award may be a man or a woman or a couple or a family or a group or a committee or a task force. In one typical example, the churchman of the week is selected by a five-person committee with a rotating membership so that either two or three members are replaced every year. A picture of the recipient appears in the church newsletter for that week accompanied by four or five descriptive paragraphs about that person or group and an explanation of why that person is being honored. A color photograph, along with the descriptive material, is mounted on a large sheet of cardboard and displayed in a prominent location in the entrance for three weeks along with similar displays prepared for the two previous recipients of this honor. In the typical year approximately one hundred and fifty to two hundred different members will be recognized either individually or as a member of a family or group or committee.

Another congregation uses the same concept, but since they do not publish a church newsletter the churchman of the week is presented with a certificate during the Sunday morning worship service.

A small rural church adapted this idea to its circumstances by presenting the certificate to the churchman of the month at the monthly Sunday evening all-church dinner.

The leaders of another congregation decided to adopt this concept, and then spent several weeks worrying about who should be the first recipient of the award and of the precedents that would be established by that first award. Finally someone said: "A week from Sunday is the twenty-fifth wedding anniversary for Fred and Mabel Curtis. While neither of them have held any major office or done anything spectacular here, they are about the most reliable and dependable two people in this church, and they never say no, regardless of what they are asked to do or who asks them. They are models of faithfulness and obedience." Later everyone in the congregation reacted to this choice with the same basic feeling: "The perfect choice! We should have done that sooner!"

The Year in Review

Another method of saying thank you to people is the celebration of the year just ended. The typical event of this type recaptures the highlights of the past year. The format varies from church to church. In one congregation a couple of enthusiastic amateur photographers capture every event on color slides. These range from weddings to the more routine activities of the congregation to a thorough coverage of the program to the local outreach of the program. At the end of the year, a few slides are borrowed from a national office to illustrate national and world missions. These are assembled to tell the story of the year, a tape is prepared to add the sound, and this presentation becomes the main event at the annual meeting. In one form or another, the contributions of every member of the congregation are identified and lifted up.

Another congregation follows a similar procedure but prepares two extra duplicate sets of slides, each with a tape cassette so that within a few days every shut-in has had the chance to see and hear the annual report.

Instead of doing this at an annual meeting, one congregation celebrates the year just ended in mid-January at a special mid-week worship service that gives thanks to God for (a) the opportunities and challenges of the past year and (b) the resources that have been given to enable them to respond to these opportunities.

In another congregation a very elaborate presentation includes color slides, skits, dramas, songs composed to recapture special events, movies, one-act plays, and other creative displays to present the year in review.

A not uncommon feature of this type of presentation is a celebration of the life and ministry of each member who died during the previous twelve months.

Four predictions can be offered with a high degree of confidence for the church that decides to have a comparatively simple celebration of the life and ministry of that congregation during the past year and uses color slides to tell the story. (These predictions are offered on the assumption that the person(s) responsible for taking the pictures is reasonably enthusiastic and consistent in fulfilling that responsibility.) First, that stack of slides will be much higher at the end of the year than anyone had anticipated. Second, a day or two after this event has been held someone who was absent will complain, "If someone had told me it was going to be that good, I would have made a point of being there; but no one told me!'' Third, the attendance the second year will be larger than it was the first year. Fourth, in preparing for that second year's event, someone will accept the responsibility to make sure that *this* year every member's face appears on that screen at least once!

The Anniversary Picnic

For more than three decades a relatively new congregation has been holding a special anniversary picnic on the third Sunday of July to celebrate its birthday. This is more than just another church picnic, however, for it includes five important and very significant dimensions.

First, each year the history of that congregation is retold from the very beginnings up to that day. Among the benefits of this are (a) remembering, recognizing, and expressing gratitude for the crucial contributions of earlier leaders, many of whom are now older ex-leaders who might otherwise be ignored by the newer leaders;[1] (b) helping the children and the new members become better acquainted with the beginnings of this congregation and thus more appreciative of the past (after hearing this story four or five times, even the recent new adult members begin to feel as if they own part of that past); (c) a clearly expressed thank-you to every member, for somewhere in this narrative—which is now a growing series of color slides—*every one of today's members is recognized either by word or by picture;* (d) the appreciation of ex-members who return for this special day and are able to see and hear what has happened since they left; and (e) reinforcing among the members the sense of purpose and purposefulness about the role of the church since this is the unifying theme for this continued story.

---

[1] This is one method of reducing the AAOEL problem described earlier, on page 39.

Second, this is a homecoming event for people who have moved away. It gives them a chance to plan their vacation travels far in advance so they can see many of their old friends at one stop. This is one reason that this event is always planned for the third weekend in July. Former members can develop their vacations around this date.

Third, it is a birthday party, and at every birthday party there are presents. In this case the members are encouraged to give an amount that is a multiple of the anniversary number for second-mile giving to missions. Thus on the twenty-seventh anniversary one child gave twenty-seven pennies while another youngster gave twenty-seven dimes and several adults gave twenty-seven ten-dollar bills for world missions.

Fourth, it is a time to celebrate the goals that were set and achieved during the past twelve months—and this reinforces the goal-setting process.

Fifth, it offers a splendid opportunity to offer a coherent preview of what is planned for the coming twelve months.

Fringe Benefits

In addition to thanking people who merit a word of gratitude for their special contributions to the life of the congregation, a systematic and intentional effort to do this usually produces five important fringe benefits.

First, and perhaps most important, it offers an excellent opportunity to lift up and affirm the purpose and distinctive role or identity of *this* congregation.

Second, by the middle of the second year it is certain that this will be a much better informed membership about the extent, depth, complexity, and quality of the life and ministry of *this* congregation. To put it in very simple terms, in most churches very few of the members know more than a tiny fraction of what is happening in that congregation. The year in review or some other method of thanking people is one way to reduce the extent of that ignorance.

Third, this is certain to raise the level of self-esteem of the congregation as a whole. As more people become more aware of what is happening in the lives of people as well as in the life of the congregation as a whole, this helps to drive away the feeling that "there is nothing happening in our church; we're about dead."

Fourth, the combination of these first three fringe benefits is almost certain to have a positive impact on the giving level of the members. To a significant degree, an individual's giving to the congregation of which he is a member reflects how much he knows about the total ministry and program of that congregation.

Finally, the congregation that systematically, intentionally, *and publicly* expresses its gratitude to the members, by name, for what they do in the life of that fellowship will make it easier for the old-timers and the newcomers to become better acquainted and to appreciate each other more as the weeks and months pass.

Some readers will still have serious objections to this whole concept of thanking people, but that misses the point. Every congregation, in one way or another, hands out both ecclesiastical Silver Beavers and dead rats to members. This is happening in your congregation! Which is handed out with the greatest degree of intentionality? Are you satisfied with the procedure, the selection process, the criteria, the value system, and the results? Those are the real questions!

5

WHAT DO THE SIGNS SAY?

About two years after Don Johnson came to St. John's as its pastor he experienced one of the most interesting issues of his ministry.

It all began shortly after his arrival, when he recognized the need to develop a response to the frequently heard complaint: This congregation was founded by young families as a church for young families back in 1951, but we're no longer able to attract young married couples! What's wrong?

This complaint had been heard with increasing frequency around St. John's for several years before Don's arrival, and the most common response was to place the blame on the pastor. This scapegoating approach is one of the most widely used techniques for problem-solving in the Christian churches on the North American continent. While it is a procedure that many church leaders, both lay and clergy, find to be very satisfying, it rarely is either creative or productive.[1]

As he sought to develop a response to this complaint Don listened very carefully at every opportunity to the comments of young couples who visited St. John's on Sunday morning. This was the first time in his career that Don had been in a situation where the church he was serving had the opportunity to reach large numbers of the people born after the end of World War II. The more he listened, the more he learned about the distinctive needs of the young married couples born in the post-1945 era.

One of the complaints he heard repeatedly from young

---

[1]For a more extensive discussion of this approach and its limitations, as well as for a more fruitful alternative, see *Hey, That's Our Church!* pp. 9-10.

mothers was that the nursery was staffed by a different person each week. Don was especially impressed by the remarks of one young couple with an eighteen-month-old baby. They had visited St. John's one Sunday morning for the first time, and the following Tuesday night Don called on them. The twenty-seven-year-old husband had been transferred by his employer from another job six hundred miles away, and neither he nor his wife had either relatives or friends in this entire metropolitan area. The first Sunday after moving into their apartment, they came to St. John's, since both had been reared in this denominational family. Don was delighted to see them back at St. John's the two Sundays following his call on them. When they did not appear on either of the two subsequent Sundays Don went to call on them again. By the time he left their apartment that evening, Don was convinced he would never again see that couple at St. John's. They had explained to Don that on the basis of their three visits to St. John's they had come away, with but one exception, with a very favorable response to that parish. They had found the people to be very friendly, the worship experience met their needs, they liked Don, they were very appreciative of his calling on them so soon after they had arrived, and St. John's was within reasonable walking distance from their apartment.

Their one objection—and this was why they were continuing to "church shop"—was that they were concerned that their daughter be encouraged to develop a very positive attitude toward church, and they did not believe this would happen at St. John's, where the nursery was staffed by a dozen mothers, each of whom took one Sunday a month and was assisted by a different teen-age girl each time. "I'm convinced that the only way we can expect Cathy to develop a strong positive attitude toward church is if she can look forward to seeing the same woman in the nursery every Sunday," explained the twenty-five-year-old mother. "After all, life is relational, and we are now learning that many of a person's attitudes and values are pretty firmly shaped by life by the time that person is three years old. We believe these next two years are very critical in Cathy's development and in her attitude toward the church for the rest of her life, and that's why we're determined to find a church where she can have a good relationship with the same adults in the nursery every Sunday.''

Don left this young couple that evening feeling very despondent. He had heard similar comments on several previous occasions. Twice he had suggested that the church hire someone to staff the nursery at St. John's on Sunday morning. In addition to the importance of the continuity of the relationships with the young children, Don urged that this was probably the only way to respond to the complaint that frequently the parents would bring their child to the nursery only to discover that the adult in charge had not yet arrived. On at least two different Sundays, owing to some unexplained mixup, the person who was scheduled to be there that Sunday never did arrive.

On each of his two previous attempts to persuade the leaders at St. John's to hire an adult to staff the nursery, Don had been unable to secure adequate support for his suggestion. ''We can't afford it,'' exclaimed a man in his fifties. ''I took my turn in the nursery when my children were little,'' responded a woman slightly older than Don, ''and I don't see why we should hire someone so these young mothers can shirk their responsibilities!'' ''Will the parents be willing to pay an extra $50 or $100 a year toward the cost of hiring someone?'' asked someone else. ''That's a part of our problem here at St. John's today. Everyone wants to hire someone else to do it rather than take their turn,'' commented another longtime member. ''I don't believe we should hire anyone for my job that can be done by volunteers,'' added another. ''Why should we ask one person to forfeit the opportunity to attend worship just to provide that kind of continuity for an hour or two? That's not fair!'' declared another of the veteran leaders.

Despite these two rebuffs, Don decided that sometime in the

future he again would propose hiring someone to staff the nursery. A couple of months later his wife Mary, mentioned to him that she had met a couple in their neighborhood who were members of a Seventh-Day Baptist church. "Why don't you ask Mrs. Cox if she would be interested in the job?" inquired his wife. "She impressed me as a very loving Christian mother. They have four children, two of whom are in college, and I have a hunch she might be interested."

A few weeks later, after talking with Mrs. David Cox and being favorably impressed with her, Don raised the issue again and suggested they hire Mrs. Cox and her sixteen-year-old daughter to staff the nursery every Sunday morning for a period beginning one-half hour before the opening of Sunday school and continuing until fifteen minutes after the end of the worship service. While there were a few questions raised about where the $600 would come from, it was decided to try this for one year.[2]

Don was surprised but pleased to see the leaders approve this proposal to staff the nursery on Sunday mornings. When he went home that evening, he believed that a minor but significant problem finally had been solved. As subsequent events would demonstrate very clearly, however, St. John's had not solved the problem. They had simply traded one problem for a different problem.

Several months later a young couple carrying a year-old baby came to St. John's one Sunday morning, and in response to their inquiry someone directed them to the nursery. As Mrs. Cox was writing down their names, the wife, who was still carrying the baby, abruptly turned and walked out announcing to her husband, "I'm not leaving my baby here!" With a somewhat startled look her husband broke off his conversation with Mrs. Cox and followed his wife out of the building to the parking lot.

[2]Why is it that a group frequently defeats a new idea the first and often the second time it is presented and then approves it very easily when it is introduced subsequently? This is explained in Lyle E. Schaller, *The Decision-Makers* (Nashville: Abingdon, 1972), pp. 19-22.

A few minutes later another young couple coming to St. John's for the first time brought their baby to the nursery. Again, as the husband was giving their names to Mrs. Cox, the wife looked around the room, clutched her baby to her, and called out, "Come on, Bill, we're not leaving Jimmy here!"

Within an hour most of the members at St. John's had heard about these two shocking incidents. Before they left the building that Sunday morning several mothers had come by to see Mrs. Cox and had agreed to meet with her in the nursery on Monday to see what was needed to renovate the nursery. As they began to prepare a list of the changes needed to make the nursery more attractive, a fifty-one-year-old woman began to cough. "I can tell you one problem we have here that some of you may not have noticed," she wheezed. "This place is moldy. I'm allergic to mold, and the mold in here is beginning to arouse my asthma!"

The following Tuesday night happened to be the regular meeting of the trustees at St. John's. Don had invited Mrs. Cox to attend. For the fifteenth time in the past fifty-six hours Mrs. Cox described what had happened on Sunday morning. When she was asked by one of the trustees what she thought should be done, she reached into her purse and pulled out a list of nearly two dozen recommendations that had been prepared by the ad hoc committee meeting on Monday afternoon.

As this list was passed from hand to hand, one of the trustees passed it along without even glancing at it and in a very belligerent tone of voice asked, "What's the issue here? Is there something wrong with the nursery? Or is there something wrong with those two couples? My wife and I joined St. John's back in the fifties when we were in our first building program. All four of our kids stayed in that nursery. If it was good enough for our kids then, I think it's probably good enough for today's crop of babies. What do these young folks expect, that we'll build them a new church to house their kids?"

By this time Mrs. Cox had recovered from the shock of

Sunday morning, and in a very gentle voice she replied, "Yes, Mr. Stephens, your wife was one of those who came over yesterday afternoon to look at the nursery. She mentioned the fact that all four of your children had spent many Sunday mornings in that nursery back in the fifties, when it was new. She also pointed out we have the same cribs, the same mattresses, the same toys, and the same equipment that was there twenty years ago, when your youngest child was a baby."

This episode raises three issues that deserve attention in every congregation seeking to reach and minister to the young married couples of today who were a part of that post–World War II "baby boom."

That First Baby

When twelve-year-old Mary Brown went to church camp for the first time her parents were somewhat apprehensive. Mary was their firstborn child and had been away from home overnight without her parents only twice before, once to a slumber party and once when she had stayed overnight with Mrs. Brown's parents. Mary's parents warned her before she left for church camp: "Now, Mary, if you have any problem or anything happens, don't hesitate to call us collect! We'll be as close as the telephone all week. If you get hurt, be sure to see the camp nurse and call us!"

A decade later the Brown's fourth child, Jimmy, went to church camp for the first time. By the time he was twelve Jimmy had been away from home overnight without his parents on many different occasions. No one, including Jimmy, knew how many times. As his father dropped him off at the church where he would get on the bus for the one hundred and sixty-mile ride to the church camp, Mr. Brown said, "Now Jimmy, if you get hurt or anything happens that you end up in the hospital and it looks as though you'll be there for a week or more, be sure to at least send us a postcard!"

While this may be an apocryphal story, it does illustrate a point of significance for church leaders in general, and especially for people born before 1935 who are anxious that their church increase the effectiveness of its ministry to people born after 1950.

What is that point? In very simple terms, it is that parents tend to be far more concerned about the health and safety of their firstborn child than about later arrivals in the family. As one father said (note it was the father, not the mother, who said it), "After the first two, having children is easy. They take care of one another." Or as someone else commented, "Having children is like murder, divorce, writing a book, or firing the preacher. After you've done it once, it's easy."

When the late 1970s are compared to the late 1950s, however, a more subtle point emerges. The change in family life-styles has meant that a far larger proportion of the babies are firstborn children. In 1960, for example, nearly one-half of the babies born had at least two older brothers or sisters, and only slightly over one-fourth (27 percent) were the first child born to that mother. Fifteen years later, more than two out of five (43 percent) of all babies were firstborns.

If one assumes that mothers tend to be less fussy about the quality of the church nursery where they drop off their second or third or fourth or fifth or subsequent child than they were when they took that firstborn child to the church nursery, the change is far greater than it appears at first glance. In 1960, 3.1 million babies were born to mothers who already had at least one child. In 1975, only 1.8 million babies were born to mothers who already had at least one child. By contrast, in 1960 there were 1.2 million mothers who that year gave birth to their first child. Despite a 25 percent decline in the total number of births over the next fifteen years, in 1975 the number of women giving birth to their first child rose to 1.4 million.

This may sound like a relatively unimportant point to the fifty-year-old trustee whose youngest child is not in high school, but it is a very significant factor to be considered by those churches seeking to reach and minister to those young couples carrying their firstborn child. More than 40 percent of the babies that were available for a second-rate church nursery in 1960 were not born in 1975.

Were You Reared in a Church Basement?

A second and closely related factor that merits consideration by those concerned with the evangelistic outreach of the church grows out of a difference in perspective. Many of the adults who helped establish new congregations such as St. John's in the decades following the end of World War II were born in the 1910–1935 era. Today the people from that generation are the most influential policy makers in tens of thousands of congregations. They control the finance committees, boards of deacons, sessions, administrative boards, church councils, vestries, consistories, voters' assemblies, boards of trustees, and general boards in thousands of small, rural churches, in hundreds of older neighborhood churches founded in the first quarter of this century, in thousands of new missions founded in the 1950s, in hundreds of "Old First Church Downtown" congregations, and in a majority of county seat churches.

Many of these church leaders born before 1935 share a very significant common characteristic. In their early years much of their time in church, especially in Sunday school, at youth meetings, and at fellowship events such as church dinners, was spent in church basements.

By contrast many of the babies born after World War II spent their formative years in the $20 billion worth of new church buildings constructed in the three decades following the close of World War II. They have been trained by their elders to appreciate and place a high value on new church buildings and to expect to find good, clean, modern, well-equipped rooms for their children in Sunday school. In many communities, especially new residential areas, this training has been reinforced by the public school system, which also has stressed the value of new, one-story buildings.

The young parents coming to St. John's had been taught by their elders to expect to find first-class physical facilities for their children. This is especially true of many young mothers bringing their first baby to the church nursery.

What Else Do They Expect?

What else do the young parents of the last quarter of the twentieth century look for when they bring their baby to the nursery at a church such as St. John's?[3]

From conversations with hundreds of these young parents it appears that many look at the quality of the physical facilities, the general housekeeping, whether there is an adult present *before* the first parents appear with their baby, and whether or not there are small children in the nursery. If these young parents have two or more children, many prefer to see nursery and kindergarten rooms located close to the rooms for the children in the lower grades: "In case Cathy seems upset, you may want to go across the hall and ask Jimmy to come over and comfort her." For reasons of health, safety, and convenience they strongly prefer to see the nursery and kindergarten rooms on the first floor rather than in the basement or on the second floor. Some inquire about a weekday nursery school with an avowedly Christian orientation and many appreciate extras, such as Parent Effectiveness Training and marriage enrichment courses for the parents or intergenerational Sunday school classes for couples with elementary-school-age children.

---

[3]For a more detailed discussion of what the young parents of today are looking for in terms of their own needs, see Lyle E. Schaller and Charles A. Tidwell, *Creative Church Administration* (Nashville: Abingdon, 1975), pp. 139-44.

What Is Reasonable?

From the perspective of the six- or eight-year-old child, a key question is, Did you really expect me to come to worship? The three most common affirmative responses to that question are (a) the children's sermon in the "adult" worship service, (b) children's church, or (c) an "alternate service" that is directed at both children and adults and is more informal and participatory in style than the traditional Sunday-morning worship service.

At this point some older adults ask: "If what you say is true, aren't some of these young parents expecting too much? We didn't expect that of the church when we brought our children to church!"

Some church leaders will respond, "Yes, these young parents are being unreasonable in their expectations!" Such a response may satisfy some of the emotional frustration of several of the older leaders; but it should be remembered that at the same time, other churches in the community are offering an affirmative response to these expectations of the young parents of today. They do not have to attend your church. They can keep looking and eventually go elsewhere!

Reading the Signs

To return to the problem Don Johnson was facing at St. John's, the trustees had too many other items on their agenda that Tuesday evening to be able to take any action on the list of recommendations that Mrs. Cox had brought to their meeting. As the time moved closer to the usual adjournment hour, they finally agreed to a special meeting on Saturday afternoon.

In preparing for this Saturday meeting Pastor Johnson decided that if the opportunity presented itself he would use a technique he had discovered at a minister's workshop.

The chairman of the trustees had expected to work through, item by item, the recommendations that Mrs. Cox had delivered to the trustees the previous Tuesday evening. When this appeared to produce more frustration than creativity, he turned to Don and asked, "Pastor, do you have any suggestions on how we should handle this?"

"I was afraid you were never going to ask," Don responded with a smile. "I think we should back off from the immediate issue of the nursery and look at the larger picture of what St. John's says to people who come here for the first time. If you remember, last October I spent five days in a minister's workshop in Memphis. One of the things I learned that week is that scattered around the meeting place of every congregation, both inside and outside the building, are posted dozens of 'signs' that are completely invisible to most of the longtime active members and barely visible to many of the more recent newcomers. These signs, however, are highly visible to many nonmembers, visitors, and potential visitors. These signs often have a tremendous impact on the expectations, attitudes, and behavior of nonmembers, neighbors, visitors, potential visitors, and newcomers to the community.

"The way they helped us grasp this concept in Memphis," continued Don, "was to ask us to walk around the half-block occupied by a large downtown church building. The largest actual existing sign around that building was the one advertising a local savings-and-loan association. The off-street parking there was both convenient and adequate for a downtown congregation, but there were only limited indications that it was acceptable for a visitor to park in what appeared to be 'a private parking lot across the valley.' From the inside of the building the directional signs suggested that only people who have been here before are expected."

As he talked Don hung on the wall several sheets of newsprint. "From my notes from that workshop I have duplicated on these sheets of paper some of the signs we identified as we walked around that downtown church building in Memphis last fall.

My hunch is that if we are willing to face reality, we will see several of these posted here at St. John's. To be more specific, I suggest we take a few minutes, go outside, walk around our property, and try to identify the signs that greet the strangers who come here to St. John's for the first time.

> THE PEOPLE WHO REG-
> ULARLY   PRACTICE
> THEIR SKILLS AT BUILD-
> ING   RELATIONSHIPS
> WITH STRANGERS WILL
> FIND THIS TO BE A VERY
> FRIENDLY, WARM, AND
> OPEN CHURCH.

I suggest that before we come back to what we're going to do about the nursery, we take a look at what we're saying to visitors of all ages and family backgrounds. Before we do

> IF YOU CANNOT WOR-
> SHIP GOD AT 11:00 A.M.
> ON SUNDAY OR PREFER
> AN   EARLIER   HOUR,
> PLEASE   GO   SOME-
> WHERE ELSE.

that, however, let me show you a sign that one of the women who came over last Monday to inspect the nursery made when she got home that afternoon. She brought it over yesterday and told me, "This is what those young couples told us last Sunday when each

> IF YOU ARE A YOUNG
> COUPLE WITH SMALL
> CHILDREN   LOOKING
> FOR A CHURCH WHICH
> HAS   WORSHIP   AND
> SUNDAY SCHOOL AT
> THE SAME HOUR—KEEP
> LOOKING!

refused to leave their baby in our nursery.' This is a woman who has been a member here at St. John's for more than a decade.''

"When she handed it to me," concluded Don, "she asked me to ask the trustees to take it down and replace it with one welcoming young parents and suggesting that we expect them here at St. John's.''

6

RETRAINING THE MEMBERSHIP

When Don Johnson arrived as the fourth pastor in the twenty-two-year history of St. John's Church, he found many committed, concerned, competent, cooperative lay leaders among the members. He also found widespread apathy, a lack of enthusiasm, low morale, declining attendance at corporate worship, the beginnings of a potential financial crisis, and a marked decline in the membership total from what it had been a few years earlier.

When Is Retraining Needed?

The need for retraining can be illustrated in general terms by looking at what happens to a great many married couples. From these two simple illustrations we can return to the pressing needs for retraining the lay leadership that Don Johnson encountered when he arrived at St. John's.

Ralph and Betty Moore had been married ten years when their first child was born. All their friends enjoyed telling them that this event would radically change their life-style, and several offered to help train Ralph for his new and more restricted role as a father. Jim Wagner had worked for the same employer for forty years when he retired on the last day on the month in which he celebrated his sixty-fifth birthday. Later, when he was asked about retirement, he responded, "The hardest part has been to retrain my wife to get used to the idea of my being around the house all day." Change usually is followed by retraining—or by frustration.

There are three major changes in the life of the typical

congregation that often produce a need to retrain congregational leadership—and if this is not done, it usually produces widespread feelings of frustration.

A Change of Pastors

When St. John's Church had passed the six hundred mark in membership, everyone assumed that this was simply another milepost on the way to becoming a one-thousand-member congregation. Instead of continuing to increase in size, however, along about year fifteen in its life St. John's hit a plateau after peaking at six hundred and eighty-three members. Seven years later, by the time Don had arrived on the scene, the membership total stood at five hundred and forty, and worship attendance was down between 10 and 15 percent from the earlier peak. Don, who is predominantly task-oriented in his leadership style, followed a minister who had been predominantly person-centered. This predecessor in turn had followed two predominantly task-oriented ministers at St. John's.

The implications of this swing of the pendulum can be seen by looking at what happened when Sam Davis came to Trinity Church following the departure of Wayne Brown. (See also pp. 43-44.) The need for a retraining program is illustrated by this episode, which paralleled, but in the opposite direction, what happened when task-oriented Don Johnson followed a person-centered minister at St. John's.

Wayne Brown was a hardworking, task-oriented, detail-conscious minister who served as pastor of Trinity Church for nine years. He enjoyed church administration, never missed a monthly board meeting, attended most of the committee meetings, and generated 90 percent of all new program ideas that were implemented at Trinity. Some members criticized him because he rarely called unless someone was sick or he knew of a specific need for a pastoral call, and others claimed that even at his best he was only an average preacher. On the other hand, many other members were delighted with his aggressive leadership. For nine consecutive years the benevolence giving at Trinity was at least 10 percent higher than the previous year, total giving more than doubled, the sanctuary was completely remodeled, and the parking lot was enlarged and paved.

Wayne was followed by Sam Davis. Sam is an excellent preacher, enjoys calling on members in their homes, hates administration, believes very strongly that church finances and the care of the church property are lay responsibilities, insists that a lay person chair the board meetings, and rarely attends any of the program committee meetings unless specifically invited. When the question of selling the ancient parsonage and buying a new one came up, he was asked his opinion. "That's up to you," was the response. "Whatever you decide to do I will support." Some members feel Sam "doesn't care," and others believe he is lazy; but many more are delighted with his excellent preaching, while others rejoice in the fact that "now we have a preacher who calls."

What does this change in pastors say to the change in the roles of lay leadership? What does it say about the retraining of lay leaders in terms of leadership roles, initiative, and expectations? If the situation had been reversed and Wayne had followed Sam, what would this say to this question of the retraining of lay leadership?

A Change in Goals

Perhaps the point in the life of a congregation when the retraining of the lay leadership becomes a most important issue is when there is a radical change in the nature of the goals or agenda of that congregation. This was the situation Don Johnson found himself in at St. John's.

St. John's Church was founded in 1953, and for the next fourteen years the agenda was dominated by building planning, building finance, and construction items. Finally the last payment on the last mortgage was made.

In anticipation of this, an all-day congregational planning meeting had been held the previous November at which the members had agreed that the top priority for the next two years should be ''the spiritual growth of the members.''

Eighteen months later a charter member commented, ''That sounded like a great idea, but today the distinctive characteristics of this congregation are apathy, declining worship attendance, factionalism, a financial crisis, and low morale.''

What had happened?

For approximately fifteen years the members of this congregation had been trained to respond to goals that were specific, achievable, measurable, tangible, highly visible, and widely satisfying. These building and financing goals also made it very easy to report to the congregation, and to the whole community, what was being planned and the progress being made in implementing those plans.

One day in November this was changed, and a new goal was adopted that was general, not specific; that was impossible to define when it was completely achieved; that could not be measured easily; that was intangible; that produced low visibility results that in fact were satisfying to less than one-third of the members.

In simple terms, the people at St. John's were not retrained when the agenda was shifted from real-estate goals to ministry goals. No effort was made to retrain the leaders, who had spent fifteen years developing task-oriented skills, in implementing a ministry-oriented agenda. In addition the internal communication system was not able to function adequately when the goals were changed from tangible and highly visible ones to intangible goals that had low visibility. This goal-less drift had continued at St. John's for another six years before Don Johnson's arrival.

A Change in Evaluation Criteria

A third example of when a retraining program becomes necessary in the life of a congregation can be illustrated by what happened at First Church.

In 1955 the leaders at First Church decided that the most important consideration in planning the educational ministry of that congregation would be *excellence*. After twenty years of (a) developing what is now widely accepted as the finest Christian education program of any of the 200 churches in this city of 140,000 residents, (b) watching the average attendance drop from 530 in 1955 to 403 in 1965 to 277 in 1976, and (c) listening to a rising wave of discontent because of the decrease in the Sunday school attendance, the educational leaders at First Church concluded that twenty years of hard and productive work would be going down the drain unless something was done to change the expectations and attitudes of the members. As these leaders began to reflect on what had happened, they realized they had shifted the programmatic emphasis from quantity to quality, broadened the focus from youth and children to an educational ministry to people of all ages, and changed from the concentration of Christian education classes on Sunday morning to a much larger number of diversified experiences scattered all through the week. There had been no comparable change, however, in the unofficial evaluation process carried out informally by the members. This informal evaluation was based almost entirely on the number of children and youth in attendance on Sunday morning without regard to what was happening during those less visible hours during the rest of the week. Many of the members were asking, "Where are all the children?" while the leaders had concluded that the key question is, "What happened to those people who did attend?"

This third change—revising the emphasis and direction of program and ministry without systematically and carefully revising the criteria used by the members in congregational self-evaluation—is perhaps the most subtle of these three changes. Therefore it *must* be accompanied by an intentional change in the evaluation criteria. Whenever expectations and performance are changed, the evaluation criteria also must be changed. This can be illustrated by what happened to Sam Davis, who followed Wayne Brown as pastor at Trinity Church. It also can be illustrated by what happened at St. John's Church and at First Church.

Rarely, however, is a congregation able to change the evaluation criteria *and have these new criteria used* unless this change is accompanied by an effort to help all members accept and use these new yardsticks in the evaluation process!

Alternatives

When a congregation finds itself facing a change in the leadership style of the pastor or a change in the nature of the goals that are at the top of the congregational agenda or a change in the value system that necessitates a change in the evaluation process, that church has at least four alternatives as it looks to the future.

The first, and the one suggested here, is a retraining program that will increase the level of competence *and self-confidence* of the laity to respond to and complement a different ministerial leadership style or cope with radically different types of congregational goals or utilize a new set of criteria in evaluating the life and ministry of the congregation.

This readjustment is unlikely to happen unless (a) the nature of the change is identified, (b) the implications of that change are recognized, (c) a retraining program is tailored to respond to those specific and distinctive needs of that unique congregation, and (d) sufficient time is allocated for this to happen.

A second alternative is to discard what appear to have become obsolete leaders and to attempt to replace them with new leaders who are comfortable in the changed situation. This unchristian alternative is attempted far more often than it is accomplished.

The third, and a far more common alternative, is to do nothing and simply allow the inevitable frustration to accumulate until people learn to live comfortably with the new reality.

Perhaps the most widespread response to the need for retraining the laity when one of these three major types of changes occurs is to search for a scapegoat. Frequently this means pointing the finger at the pastor, and, instead of retraining the laity, the decision is made to seek a new minister. This search for a messiah is part of the history of nearly every long-established congregation and may be the greatest single barrier to developing widespread acceptance of the need for retraining of the laity.

7

WHAT DO WE LOOK LIKE TO YOU?

"I enjoy meeting with you all every week," drawled the Reverend Robert Wilcox, rector of Trinity Episcopal Church, "but I believe we should have a better organized agenda for this ministerial fellowship. About half the time we do some productive studying or have a provocative speaker; it's the other half of these Thursday mornings I'm talking about."

"That's two of us," agreed the Reverend Harold Phelps, pastor of the Northminster Presbyterian Church. "I enjoy living here in Danville. I enjoy being the pastor of my congregation, and I enjoy this ministerial fellowship; but I think we ought to have a project or goal beyond fellowship and occasional study. What can we do to help one another, to help our congregations, and to strengthen our Christian witness?"

"Let me offer a suggestion," responded Pastor Ken Anderson from St. Paul's Lutheran Church. "Why don't we spend a week on the community image of each of our congregations? Next week, for example, you guys can tell me how you see St. Paul's. From an outside perspective, what are your perceptions of my parish? How do other folks here in Danville see St. Paul's? What's our image in this community? I've been here three years and I see our parish from the inside. What does it look like from the outside, to nonmembers? I'm convinced we all would be helped if we had a clearer understanding of the community image of our congregations. To accomplish this will require that we be honest rather than polite with one another and that we really level with one another!"

"This sounds like a great idea to me," observed the Reverend Gerald Wilson from Wesley United Methodist Church, "but I believe we should do it in two stages. Let's have one round where the clergy does this. After we finish looking at each congregation I would like to schedule a second round where we invite the laity in to tell us what they see when they look at these nine churches.''

After another twenty minutes of discussion it was agreed that for each of the next nine Thursday mornings, forty-five minutes of the session would be devoted to describing what these ministers perceived to be the identity of one of the nine congregations represented in this ministerial fellowship. It was also agreed that four ground rules would apply. First, the pastor of the congregation being described that morning would be limited to two sets of comments. He could respond to requests for factual information, and he could ask anyone present to expand or elaborate on a comment or statement; but he could not challenge any statement of fact, opinion, or interpretation. This was agreed on to avoid placing a pastor in a defensive position. Second, no church would be discussed unless the pastor was present for the discussion. If a minister had to be absent when the week came to discuss his church, that discussion would be postponed until he could be present. Third, the first round of discussions with only the ministers present was to be treated as confidential and not carried back to the churches. Fourth, to encourage uninhibited discussion when the laity were involved, no lay persons from the church being discussed would be invited that week.

The Maple Avenue Christian Church was the subject of the first week's discussion. Among the descriptive comments offered that day were these. "The most vivid image I have of that congregation is that the leaders include a number of preacher's kids; I doubt if any other church in town has as many P.K.s" "I'm impressed," commented another minister, "by the number of members who are involved in denominational affairs on both the state and national levels." "I guess the clearest image I have is one that goes back about twenty-five years when the minister and a small group of members walked out to form the independent Northside Christian Church.'' ''I'm comparatively new in town, and I guess about all I know reflects what I see in and have learned from the minister.'' ''My image is one of a core of very, very loyal members.'' ''When I exchanged pulpits with Bill,'' notes another pastor, ''I was surprised to see such a small choir; I doubt if there were more than eight or ten in the choir that Sunday.'' ''My view of Maple Avenue is of a congregation that is overwhelmingly self-centered, and the handful of people who are interested in community ministries and outreach into Danville stands out as an exception to the general pattern of congregational behavior and values.'' ''When I hear any of my members talk about Maple Avenue, about half of the time the reference is to Bill's predecessor, who came right after the split and was a very loving and reconciling minister. I guess he stayed about fifteen or twenty years, didn't he?'' ''I see a middle middle-class congregation with a handful of highly visible members in the professions and practically no factory workers or unskilled workers.''

The following week the Pilgrim United Church of Christ was the focus of the discussion among the ministers. ''It used to be the most prestigious congregation in town, but now it's tied for second place with Trinity Episcopal and far behind Northminster Presbyterian.'' ''The organist–choir director and the music program come through to me more clearly than anything else.'' ''I am impressed by the number of women in key leadership positions.'' ''The other side of that is when I exchanged pulpits with Glenn,'' commented another minister. ''I was depressed by the proportion of women to men in the congregation. I'll bet that at least 70 or 75 percent of the people present for worship that Sunday morning were females.'' ''The only image I have is of the building; it's right off a calendar, especially in the winter when there is lots of snow on the ground.'' ''I hadn't thought of this until I was going home after last week's discussion,'' declared Pastor Ken Anderson, "but we have had a number of our young people marry someone from Pilgrim. When I got back to the office I went through our membership records and found nineteen marriages between a member of St. Paul's Lutheran and a member from Pilgrim Congregational Church. Seven of these couples have moved out of Danville and all seven transferred to a Lutheran church in the community to which they moved. Of the other twelve, nine couples are members of St. Paul's, one couple is at Pilgrim, one couple went to Maple Avenue Christian Church, and I don't know where the other couple went. Does that say anything about what Pilgrim is teaching its young people?" "I guess my dominant image is of an older, upper- and upper-middle-class, fairly well-to-do, theologically liberal but socially and politically conservative congregation that is beginning to grow old and gradually diminishing in size."

After nine weeks of asking the ministers to describe the community image of each of the participating congregations, the Danville Ministerial Association invited a different group of seven to twelve lay persons to come in for each of the following nine weeks and identify what they saw as the distinctive characteristics of the congregation that was on the agenda for that week. Among the comments offered by the lay people at these sessions were these.

"What do I see when you ask me about Trinity Episcopal Church?" asked a widely known community leader in Danville. "While I'm not a member there, I do know a lot of people who are members there, and I guess the outstanding characteristic of that congregation is the building. It's one of the outstanding architectural landmarks in this city."

"When Pastor Johnson asked me to come over this morning and share my image of Bethel Church, I was very embarrassed," confessed a member from St. John's. "While I haven't admitted this to anyone before, I didn't know which church in town was Bethel. I looked it up in the telephone book and discovered that I have driven past it hundreds of times since we moved here, but I didn't know it. I guess maybe that says more about me than about the church.''

"I suspect that the Arlington Church is best known here for its dinners. They have a big ham dinner in the spring and a chicken dinner in the summer. I suppose you could meet half the people in town if you went to their turkey dinner in the fall. That's always a sellout, I guess.'' This was the response of a Presbyterian in Danville when he was asked about the community image projected by Arlington Church.

"That's an easy question," responded a Lutheran when she was asked about Park Place Church. "While I'm not a member there, I believe everyone in town would agree that Park Place leads every other church in town in its emphasis on community ministries. If you have a few minutes to spare, I'll be glad to tell you about some of the things they're doing, but I'm sure my list will be far from complete.''

"What comes to my mind when you say 'Northminster Church' to me? That's easy! The minister. He is one of the half-dozen best-known leaders in this city." This was the reply of a Baptist laywoman.

"Bethel Church? I guess they're best known here for their revivals," commented a Methodist layman. "Every spring and fall they bring in a big-name preacher for a week of revival meetings.''

"When I think about St. John's, I see a solid, tradition-oriented church that isn't going to collapse, but probably won't be doing anything radical or spectacular. I don't want to use the word conservative, because I don't believe that's quite the word," reflected a member from Trinity Episcopal. "The other thing that comes to mind is the Reverend Donald Johnson. Mr. Johnson is the first minister to serve St. John's that I have ever come to know personally, and I guess today the community image of St. John's is carried as much for me by the minister as by the congregation.''

This list could go on and on. One congregation's local fame rested on its excellent choir, another was best known among the laity for its huge Sunday school, the community image of a third was built on great preaching, a fourth was known for the prominence of its members in community affairs, and the local reputation of a fifth congregation rested on its interest in and support of foreign missions. One congregation was known for never letting a minister stay more than two or three years, while another congregation was identified as the "splinter church" because three other congregations have formed as a result of splinter groups leaving it to organize new churches. Several lay persons agreed that the dominant community image of one congregation was its reputed excellence in its ministry to youth, and another group identified one congregation primarily from its buses that picked up children from all sections of the Danville area to take them to its Sunday school.

Why Ask?

There are at least five reasons that the leaders of every congregation should ask themselves the question, What is the identity or community image perceived by outsiders when they look at our church?

One of the most important reasons is that change and the passage of time bring a challenge to the traditional identity of the institution. Two examples of this can be seen in what the coming of the metric system has done to the self-image of the inchworm and what the elimination of polio has done to the traditional image of the March of Dimes. Or consider the congregation that was founded to serve a specific neighborhood in 1922, but today less than 15 percent of the members live within a mile and a half of the building. Another example is the congregation that has always characterized itself as a family church, but today 20 percent of the members live in one-person households and another 55 percent of the members live in one-generation households. If the congregational self-image does not coincide with reality it will be difficult to project an inviting image to the community.

Whether the subject be automobiles, presidential candidates, banks, physicians, colleges, or churches, the response of many individuals is determined largely by the image perceived by people of that institution, product, or person. Change often requires a deliberate effort to project a new image.

A closely related and more important reason for asking this question is to discover if the image that is held by others is the image your congregation wants to project. It is not uncommon, for example, for the leaders of a congregation to be both surprised and disappointed when they discover that others use words such as *exclusive, wealthy,* and *prestigious* when describing their congregation. It is less common, but not unusual, for outsiders to describe a congreagation in terms of the minister—but that pastor left four or five years earlier! Since his departure the community image of that congregation has been only a vague blur. In another case, outsiders saw one congregation as torn by strife and factionalism, but those divisions had been healed for years. Frequently, outsiders describe a congregation as cold, aloof, or unfriendly, while the members see themselves as a very friendly congregation.

Unquestionably, the most important reason for asking this question concerns the evangelistic outreach of the church. The vast majority of growing congregations project a clear identity of who they are and what they are trying to do in ministry and outreach. Congregations that project a blurred or vague image or identity tend to be congregations that are not reaching new people and often they are declining in size. The congregations that are perceived as being in the midst of an identity crisis tend to repel rather than to attract people.

A fourth reason for asking this question is related to self-evaluation and can be described most easily by the use of categories. The identity or image projected into the community by a congregation tends to fall into one of four categories—pastor, property, people (members or congregational leaders), or program.

Which of these four categories is the one you believe should reflect the way outsiders view your congregation? Property? Pastor? People? Program? Which one of these categories matches most closely your understanding of the biblical nature of the Christian church?

Finally, discovering the identity projected by your congregation often will be helpful in evaluating the precision and clarity of the congregational goals. The congregations that can be identified and described by nonmembers with the greatest clarity and accuracy usually are those which are responding to a widely understood set of precisely defined goals.

What Happens Next?

After the ministerial association had completed this effort to help each congregation discover its image in the community, Pastor Don Johnson brought together the eight people from St. John's who had shared in this experience. Three of the eight had participated in either two or three of the meetings with the ministers. "What did we learn from this experience?" asked Don to open the discussion.

"It certainly was a consciousness-raising experience for me," responded Dorothy Morris. "I am much more conscious of the existence of the other churches here in Danville than I ever was before. Whether I'm driving around town, reading the paper, or talking with friends, I certainly am aware of the churches and subconsciously trying to identify the distinctive characteristics of each one. I was at the session when we talked about the Arlington Church, and I learned some things I didn't know that day; but I've learned a lot more since. That was a kind of a training experience for me."

"I'm still embarrassed over how little I had to share," offered Ira Ward, "When Don asked me to go to the session where Bethel Chruch would be discussed, I didn't even know which church was Bethel. When I looked it up, I discovered that the building owned by Bethel was what I had thought was the Church of the Brethren building."

"That's interesting," commented Rollie Patterson. "I wonder how many people in Danville know which building is the meeting place for St. John's."

"My hunch is that a lot more know who we are since we put up the big sign out front," declared Jack McIntire. "A number of people at work have told me that they wondered why we waited nearly twenty-five years before we put up a sign that could be read by people going by in a car."

"From what you're saying," said Don, "I gather that you see the community image of a church primarily in terms of the property. Is that what you're saying?"

"I think that's only the beginning point," replied Agnes Peterson. "I believe we do begin to identify churches by the property, but as we get better acquainted we begin to identify a church by the people who are members. I'm sure that many people here in Danville would describe St. John's as a friendly church because they know the members here."

"That's interesting," observed Don. "There were eleven lay persons from seven other churches there the day we focused on St. John's and not a one used the word *friendly,* or anything close to it, in describing the community image of St. John's."

"That's incredible!" exclaimed Grace Brandt. "How did they describe us?"

"I think I can summarize what they said in four words," replied Pastor Johnson. "The first word is vague. Most of the eleven were vague—and a couple were very vague—about St. John's. When asked, three of them said they didn't even know our denominational label, and one who thought she knew was

wrong. The other three words are *property, people,* and *pastor.*
Only one comment was offered about our community image that
reflected our ministry and program or what we do as a
congregation. It was a rather disillusioning experience for me."

"Well, wasn't that true of all the other churches?" inquired
Dr. Lewandowski in a defensive tone of voice. "Weren't people
pretty vague about the ministry and program of the other
churches?"

"No," replied Don. "The lay people who participated in this
were surprisingly knowledgeable and accurate about the distinctive programs and ministries and characteristics of four
congregations. They were almost completely ignorant about two
and vague about three. St. John's was one of the three. The few
perceptive and informed comments that were offered about St.
John's were out of date by five to ten years."

"What does that say to us here at St. John's?" asked Dorothy
Morris with some anxiety in her voice. "What are we doing or
not doing that should be corrected?"

"I was at the session when we discussed Park Place Church,"
commented Roger Ellsworth. "I was very highly impressed by
how clearly the outsiders saw that church's community
outreach, the theological stance of the congregation, and various
other aspects of the ministry and program of that church. Very
little was said about a community image based on real estate; it
was almost entirely on what that congregation is doing and on
the membership. A little was said about the minister, but most of
the discussion was on program and outreach."

"What does that say to us here at St. John's?" asked Grace
Brandt.

"Maybe it says we are not doing much that the rest of the
community is aware of, or else we're remarkably effective at
keeping secret what we are doing," responded Jack McIntire.

"Or maybe it says that we at St. John's aren't doing anything
distinctive or unique or special," suggested Dorothy Morris.

"Maybe we should begin to develop one or more specialities in ministry and outreach that will sharpen our identity in people's minds." [1]

Three Alternative Approaches

Some congregations will not be able to use the approaches described here as they seek to discover how the rest of the community sees their church. An alternative approach that has been used by many congregations is to focus on new members. One Midwestern Presbyterian congregation, for example, asks each prospective adult member to respond to these five questions when the prospective members meet with the session.

1. Why did you pick this church? What were the reasons, persons, events, or circumstances that caused you to come here the first time?
2. What kept you coming back?
3. What do you see as the strongest point in the total life, ministry, and program of this congregation?
4. What turns you off about this church? What is it you do not like or that you disapprove of here?
5. What suggestion(s) do you have to offer that might help us improve what we're doing or how we are doing it here in this church?

While this procedure tends to give the members of the session an unusually favorable description of how newcomers or outsiders see their church—the visitors or potential new members who visited once or twice and then decided to join a different church are not interviewed—it is an enlightening experience for the members of the session.

---

[1] For an elaboration of the concept that every congregation should have at least one specialty in ministry see Lyle E. Schaller, *Hey, That's Our Church!*, pp. 137-41.

A better but far more difficult procedure is followed by one congregation, which has an effective system for identifying all visitors. Twice a year a committee checks the list of visitors, and each committee member calls on two or three persons or families from that list who have united with that congregation. Questions similar to those used by the Presbyterian church mentioned earlier are used by the caller in this visit. Next, the committee circulates the remaining names on the list to a dozen other churches in town and asks them to check the names of the people who are new members or prospective new members. Members of the committee then call on each of these households and, without any effort to proselytize, attempt to discover what happened that caused these people to seek out another congregation after visiting their church. This gives that committee a twice-a-year view of what was perceived by visitors who came and stayed and also by the visitors who came and then continued to church shop.

A third alternative is to ask someone (not the pastor!) to conduct an "exit interview" with every member who is leaving, whether that person is moving to another community or remaining within the community and transferring to another church. If given the opportunity and encouraged to go beyond the veneer of polite conversation, they may have detailed comments, both favorable and unfavorable, about the identity projected by your congregation. (As you pursue any of these suggested approaches to discovering how others see your church, it may be helpful to keep in mind John 8:32.)

8

WHY DIDN'T YOU CALL ON MY MOTHER?

"This may sound like I'm trying to mind your business, Pastor," hesitantly suggested Mrs. Carleton to the Reverend Don Johnson, "But if I were you, I'd make it a point to stop by and see Tom Swartz at the first opportunity. He seems to be upset that you've been ignoring his mother. Please don't say I sent you, but I believe it's important that you hear how he feels. That's all I'd better say."

While he was completely mystified by this piece of advice from one of his strongest supporters at St. John's, Pastor Johnson made it a point to drop in on Mr. and Mrs. Tom Swartz that very evening. After several minutes of small talk, Don recognized that Tom Swartz was coldly formal rather than the friendly and gregarious person Don had become acquainted with two years earlier when the Swartz family moved to town and transferred their membership to St. John's.

"While I hope I'm wrong, I'm sorry to see that your mother doesn't seem to be improving. When I was in to see her this morning she seemed to be her old self every once in awhile, but most of the time she appeared to be almost in a coma," ventured Don. "Day before yesterday when I was coming out of her room, I bumped into Dr. Leary; and while he was pretty guarded in his comments, he didn't seem to be very optimistic about a quick recovery. What does he tell you?"

"You're telling me you were in to see my mother the day before yesterday and again this morning?" asked Mr. Swartz in a grim voice.

"Why, yes," replied Don Johnson very innocently. "I must

123

confess I don't get to the hospital every day, but since most of our people go to Riverside General, where your mother is, I do get in to see her four or five times a week. Let's see, today is Friday, so I saw her Saturday, Monday, Wednesday, Thursday, and today. Tuesday is my day off, so I didn't get to the hospital; and I guess I won't make it tomorrow, but I'll probably stop by Sunday. Rarely do two consecutive days go by that I don't get to Riverside General since we usually have two or three or four of our members there on any given day."

"That's strange," replied Tom, still without any warmth in his voice. "We get in to see Mother nearly every day, and her most common complaint is the pastor doesn't come to call on her. She's asked me at least a dozen times to call you and ask you to visit her. I've hesitated to call you because I know you're busy, but I thought you should be able to stop by and see her at least once a week. After all, she's been a member of this congregation for over fifteen years."

"Let's stop and talk about this," urged Don. "Obviously there's been some mix-up. I've been in to see your mother on at least two or three occasions when both you and your wife were in the room; so you know for a fact that I haven't neglected your mother completely. On several other occasions, when I wasn't sure your mother was herself, I left my card on the table by the bed so she would remember that I was there and be reassured that she was in our thoughts and prayers."

"In all my visits to the hospital—and sometimes I get over there two or three times a day—I've never seen any of your calling cards on the table," declared an obviously skeptical Tom Swartz.

"Maybe the nurses pick them up and throw them away," suggested Mrs. Swartz. "Or maybe they put them in the drawer and we just never see them."

"All I can say is that I've been in to see her four or five times a week ever since she entered the hospital," responded Don with some sense of relief that he had finally discovered what was troubling Tom Swartz, but at a loss as to what to do next.

"That's a pretty tough choice you're offering me," replied Tom Swartz thoughtfully. "Do I believe my pastor, or do I believe my mother?"

Malpractice Insurance

The Reverend Don Johnson had been caught in the same trap that has caught hundreds of other pastors, many of whom never did discover what had alienated one of their parishioners. In each case the pastor faithfully and regularly visited an older church member, but the combination of age and illness caused these visits to fade very rapidly from the memory of that member. A few hours later a son or daughter hears the complaint, "Why doesn't our minister ever visit me?" After hearing this complaint a dozen or a score of times, it is hard for that son or daughter not to begin to have some doubts about their pastor's faithfulness.

Back in the days when a three-cent stamp only cost a dime, one pastor, after having been caught in this predicament with two different families, made it a point to send a brief note to the son or the daughter after every visit to each of his older parishioners, whether that person was in the hospital, a nursing home, or a home for retired persons. When a ministerial friend heard that he was spending an hour or two and two or three dollars every week on this practice, he challenged him, "How can you justify spending that much time and money every week doing this?" "It's cheaper than malpractice insurance," was the immediate reply. For many pastors that illustrates the choices: quietly and faithfully calling on the old and the sick and taking the risk of being accused, often without ever knowing the accusation is being made, of not calling; or spending the time and money on letting the close relatives know that their pastor is tending his flock. The large number of volunteer martyrs among the clergy guarantees the first option is followed more often than the second.

An entirely different response to the same type of problem was developed by another minister. In his first year as a parish pastor this minister had developed the habit of inquiring about the individual's health, work, hobby, favorite ball team, or vacation whenever he met one of his members and had a few seconds for conversation. He reasoned that it was better to begin every conversation with the other person's agenda than to yield to the temptation to begin with his own or with a churchy agenda.

After three different disasters, he changed his style. The first problem paralleled what had happened to Don Johnson. The daughter of an elderly member began to circulate the rumor: "I don't know why our minister doesn't want to call in nursing homes. Mother says he hasn't been in to see her for more than six months." Eventually the rumor reached this minister, who called on every member in a nursing home at least once a month; but his denials were of little value in combating a rumor that had been circulating for months. Sometime later he agreed to perform the wedding for the son of a leading member, although neither the son nor his bride were or ever had been a member of the congregation he was serving. Twenty months later he happened to ask the mother of the bridegroom, "What do you hear from your son and his wife?" The reply was delivered in an icy tone of voice, "Oh, didn't you know? They were divorced last fall." The third episode involved the son of a family who had moved to town with the parents transferring their membership to the congregation he served. The son had dropped out of church completely a few years earlier and did not ask to have his membership transferred. A couple of years later this pastor inquired, "Your son Dick will be ready to graduate from the university soon, won't he?" Again the reply was delivered wrapped in a chunk of ice: "Tom was dropped from the university a year and a half ago, and he's in the Army now and stationed in Germany.''

After discovering that most people do not volunteer unhappy news about their kinfolk, this minister now automatically begins most conversations with questions such as, ''What do you hear from your son [mother, father, sister, brother, daughter, uncle, aunt, etc.]?'' Or with a comment such as, ''Last week when I visited your father in the nursing home . . .'' or ''Yesterday when I saw your mother in the hospital . . .'' or ''The other day I got to wondering whatever happened to your son Jeff and his wife . . .'' or ''I saw your brother going into the post office last week but I didn't get a chance to talk to him. How is he?'' By this modest change in his method of greeting people, this minister now has members volunteering information that enables him to be a far more effective pastor.

What Is a Call?

''If you folks will tell me what you understand constitutes a call, I'll be glad to make a monthly report on my calling,'' offered the Reverend Don Johnson as the church council once again drifted over to the subject of how much calling Don did and how much was needed.

Don had come to St. John's as the pastor nearly six years earlier. During that first year he had made a conspicuous point of calling in every home in this five-hundred and forty-member congregation. As the years passed, however, his calling became less systematic and less visible. Gradually Don began to hear more and more negative comments about his calling or lack of it.

It appeared that the matter might come to a head tonight at the church council when Milt Wilcox suggested that he submit a monthly report on the number of calls he had made. When Milt made this suggestion in what several others perceived as a critical, rude, and demanding tone of voice, George Merrill quickly stepped in and in a soothing voice added: "Please don't consider this as a judgment or a criticism, Pastor. The problem that Milt and the rest of us have is that when people come to us and complain that you're not doing enough calling, we aren't equipped to defend you. For example, I know you spend considerable time calling, but if I knew how many calls you were making, I would be in a better position to help some of the critics understand that you are doing your job."

"That's all we're asking," added Jane McVey. "If you would give us a simple statement every month, it could keep a few minor complaints from growing into a real problem. All we're asking for is a three-line report. How many home calls did you make last month? How many hospital calls did you make last month? What is the total? My father was a Presbyterian minister for over forty years, and I know he did this every month for the session. I don't believe we're asking for anything unreasonable."

It was at this point that Pastor Johnson raised his question about the definition of a call. "Let me give you three examples," he added. "Several weeks ago I stood out in the parking lot for over an hour one evening after one of our fellowship dinners counseling with a couple in this congregation about their daughter. Should that count as a call? I accomplished as much or more in terms of pastoral care as I could have if I had spent an hour in their home. Last week I spent close to an hour on the steps of the library talking with one of our high-school seniors about the choice he is faced with between taking a very attractive job or going to college. If he decides to go to college in the fall, he won't get this job, and he may not be able to get any kind of decent summer employment. Just the other day I spent thirty minutes at the Y being introduced to a newcomer to this community. As a result of that introduction through a mutual acquaintance who is *not* a member of this congregation, that man and his wife were in church here last Sunday and they have expressed an interest in transferring their membership to St. John's. Do you want me to count those as calls? They were neither home calls nor hospital calls. In addition, during the typical week I make at least a dozen "pastoral calls" on people who come to see me in my office here in the church."

"Well, maybe the job of a minister here at St. John's today is different from what it was a generation ago in rural America," conceded Jane McVey. "Maybe we should ask for a five-line report: home, hospital, office, other, and total. I agree that the three illustrations you just offered should be counted as legitimate pastoral calls, and I don't see any reason that they can't be included in a monthly report."

"Let me try one more question on you," persisted Pastor Johnson. "Last week Pete Garcia was admitted to the hospital on Tuesday afternoon. I stopped by that evening and spent five or six minutes with him. The next morning I was over at the hospital at 7:15 A.M. to pray with him before he was taken to the operating room. Then I spent the next three hours with Mrs. Garcia and their daughter waiting for Pete to come back from the operating room. I then went with them and spent an hour with them and Pete in the recovery room. I believe you would want me to count that brief Tuesday evening visit as one hospital call, but do you want me to count Wednesday morning as one call, two calls, or three calls? It seems a little deceptive in reporting to count five minutes as one call and to count five hours as one or even two or three calls."

"Everyone agrees you're great on hospital calling," interrupted George Merrill. "It's the home calling, or the lack of it, that seems to have people upset. We know you spend a lot of time with the sick and at the hospital. That's great, but that's a different subject. What we need is your help in responding to those people who criticize your lack of home calling."

"As I think you all can see, I'm getting fed up with this bickering about my calling. It's not simply that I'm thin-skinned and can't take criticism; this subject takes up time at church council meetings that should be spent on more important matters," declared Don impatiently. "I'm ready to strike a bargain with you. If you will promise not to bring up this subject of my calling at any church council meeting during the next twelve months, I'll promise to call in every home at least once during the next year."

"That's a deal, Pastor!" exclaimed Milt Wilcox. "A year from now, at our church council meeting next June, this will be on the agenda; but I promise you that I won't say a thing about it between now and next June. Furthermore I'll lean pretty hard on anyone else who tries to bring it up between now and then!"

Calling in Every Home

The following Sunday this notice appeared in the church bulletin at St. John's: "The Pastor has promised the church council that he will call on every home at least once during the next twelve months. There are 316 households represented in the membership of this congregation; so that means an average of six home calls per week."

A week later this notice was in the bulletin at St. John's.

CALLS BY PASTOR—JULY TO JUNE

Member home calls to be on schedule	6
Member home calls completed to date	5
"Second round" member home calls to date	0
Nonmember home calls to date	2
Hospital calls to date	7
Office pastoral care visits	11
Other pastoral care visits	4
Total pastoral care visits to date	29

Two and a half months later, and a couple of weeks after Don and Mary had returned from a three-week vacation in August, this box score appeared in the Sunday bulletin at St. John's.

CALLS BY PASTOR—JULY TO JUNE

Member home calls to be on schedule	66
Member home calls completed to date	43
"Second round" member home calls to date	12
Nonmember home calls to date	26
Hospital calls to date	55
Office pastoral care visits	61
Other pastoral care visits	28
Total pastoral care visits to date	225

Every Sunday this box score appeared in the bulletin at St. John's. Within a month or two everyone understood that this was the weekly report on the pastor's promise that he would call in every home in St. John's parish during this twelve-month period. Each week the top line of the box score reported the number of calls on members in their homes necessary to have been completed by this date if Pastor Johnson was to meet this schedule of an average of six home calls on members per week. The second line reported the number of home calls on members Don had completed thus far in this race against the calendar.

For many of the members at St. John's, this two-line weekly report would have been all they expected or wanted. Don had decided, however, that since the question of his calling had been turned into a major issue at St. John's he would not stop with this oversimple descriptive report. He decided he would take advantage of this opportunity to help the members understand the variety and complexity of pastoral care in a contemporary urban parish. Therefore he added six more lines to the weekly box score in the bulletin.

The third line, which he called "second round" calls on members in their homes, reported the number of home calls he had completed where this was the second or third or fourth time he had called in that home since he had begun this effort to call in every member's home. If he did not include these in that weekly box score, he would be deceiving the people on the amount of home calling he was actually doing.

Don had two reasons for including the fourth line about home calls on nonmembers. The more important was that he did not want to reinforce the widely held belief that his job was to be concerned only with members. He wanted to legitimate his responsibility as a pastor to nonmembers, some of whom might be prospective members but some of whom would never unite with St. John's. The second reason for including this line was to offer a more comprehensive report on the number and variety of calls made by the pastor.

The fifth line was a direct response to Jane McVey's request for a regular report on the minister's hospital calling. Here Don simply reported the number of hospital calls he made thus far in this highly publicized year of pastoral calling.

The next two lines reported what Pastor Johnson sometimes referred to as his low-visibility calling. The sixth line reported the number of pastoral care visits carried out in Don's office at the church, while the seventh line represented the informal and often completely spontaneous pastoral care visits with people in the church parking lot, on the steps of the library, over a cup of coffee in the restaurant, in a member's office or place of work, on a street corner, in a nursing home, or at the lake. Here again Don was using these two categories to help the members understand that the pastoral care of people took place in settings other than the home or the hospital.

The last line reported the total number of pastoral visits by the minister. In developing this box score, Don had decided that if the members insisted on a statistical report on his calling they would get a complete box score with the total to date reported very clearly. He had enough businessmen in his congregation who were bottom-line-oriented that he recognized the importance of including a grand total figure as the last item in the box score.

Fifty-one weeks after Don had gone out on the limb in declaring that he would call in every home in the parish during the next year, and the Sunday before the June meeting of the church council at St. John's, this box score appeared in the bulletin.

CALLS BY PASTOR—JULY TO JUNE

Member homes in the congregation	321 *
Number of different member homes visited by the pastor	321
"Second round" member home calls for one year	202
Nonmember home calls for one year	177
Hospital calls for one year	388
Office pastoral care visits for one year	313
Other pastoral care visits for one year	264
TOTAL PASTORAL CARE VISITS FOR ONE YEAR	1,665

*There was a net increase of five member households during the year.

The following Tuesday evening at the church council Milt Wilcox shook Don's hand with delight and declared, "I knew if you set your mind to it, Pastor, you could get your priorities straightened out and do the calling we all expect of our minister!"

George Merrill added: "We kept our part of the bargain, Don, and you certainly kept your part! I'm a little ashamed of myself, however, for it was easy for us to refrain from bringing this up at council meetings. It's been at least six to eight months since I heard the last complaint about your not calling, and for several weeks all I've heard is what a great job you're doing in your calling."

"That's the same with me, Pastor," chimed in Jane McVey. "Everyone is highly impressed with the amount of calling you've done during the past year. Last week I was at our garden club meeting, and two of our members were bragging to the rest about how much calling our minister does.''

''Is it your understanding that the discontent about my not doing enough calling has pretty well disappeared?'' Don asked the members of the church council after everyone had arrived. They all agreed that not only had the discontent disappeared, but that most people were delighted with the amount of calling the minister was doing.

''I would like to close this discussion with three observations before we go on to the next item of business,'' suggested Don. ''During the seven years I have been here as your pastor, as a matter of self-discipline, I have kept reasonably accurate records on how I spend my time. First, I don't believe there is any question but that I spent more time calling in my first year here than in any subsequent year. Second, as near as I can tell, I did not spend any more time calling or make any more calls this past year than I had made in the previous two or three years when you and I heard so many complaints about the lack of pastoral calling. Third, the major change between this past year and the previous years was not in the amount of calling I did, but rather that I was a little more careful and systematic about making sure I got into every home during the year; and by reporting my calls in this box score in the church bulletin every Sunday I gave a lot more visibility to my calling and the pastoral care of people. I didn't spend any more time calling, I just stopped keeping it a secret.''

''That's fascinating, simply fascinating!'' commented George Merrill.

9

EXPAND OR CUT BACK?

"We have a wonderful pastor, a fine building, and an outstanding choir, and this is such a friendly congregation, I can't understand why we're not growing, Pastor," complained a member of the Memberhip and Evangelism Committee at St. John's with great frustration. "But instead of growing, our numbers are getting smaller. Every year our membership declines, and we have fewer people in church. I simply can't understand why more people don't come here. It seems that today people aren't interested in church the way they were twenty years ago when we were just getting started here. What's wrong with those people? Why don't they come to church?"

These comments were offered one evening at a meeting of the Membership and Evangelism Committee about three years after Don Johnson had arrived as the pastor of that congregation.

"Now, Rose, you know that's not an accurate statement," responded Dean Hiller, who chaired that committee. "It's true that we're not as large as we were ten years ago, but I think we've reversed the direction. The worship attendance and membership have both increased since Don came. I think we're moving into a new era. Don't be so pessimistic! Be a little more optimistic!"

"I'm somewhat inclined to agree with Rose," commented Betty Rhodes. "My husband and I came to St. John's back in 1955, and while we're not charter members, we have been here longer than most people. I can remember back in the 1960s when we were talking about becoming a one-thousand-member congregation by 1978. That's turned out to be a dream! But the people are here. While the population growth in this suburb has not kept up to the projections of fifteen years ago, the community is growing. New people are moving in every week. I'm like Rose—why aren't we growing? It's true we have begun to grow a little since Don came as our pastor, but we're still not up to where we were back in 1968 and 1969. Why? Why can't we reach more of these newcomers? My neighbor goes to Grace Community Church, and they've doubled in size during the past years. Why hasn't St. John's grown more? What's wrong with us?''

As he listened to this discussion, Pastor Don Johnson decided that Betty's last question offered him the best entry point that was likely to come along for him to get into this discussion.

"Let's compare what Rose said with what you just said, Betty," he began. "Rose asked us what's wrong with the people out there who aren't coming to St. John's. Betty asked just the opposite question—what's wrong with *us* that more newcomers to the community aren't finding their way to St. John's. I'm as distressed about this as any of you. When I came here nearly three years ago, I expected this could and would be an evangelistic congregation and that St. John's would be up to seven hundred or more members by now.''

"We're not blaming you, Pastor," interrupted Dean Hiller. "I'm sure everyone is happy with your work here. It's just a part of the age we live in. People aren't as interested in the church as they were back in the 1950s.''

"I'm not interested in placing the blame on anyone or in searching for a scapegoat," replied Don. "I think we ought to take Betty's question seriously. What's wrong with us as a congregation? If we can focus on what we do or don't do, we have control over that. If we talk about what's wrong with other people, we've lost control of the situation. We don't have control over what other people do or don't do. All we have control over is what we do or don't do, so let's concentrate on that. Now, what are we doing or not doing that keeps people from uniting with this congregation?''

With this question Don pointed the committee in the direction of seeking to discover how St. John's had become an exclusionary congregation.

Seven Barriers to Growth

Most congregations tend to become exclusionary (without ever intending for that to happen) and gradually create barriers to any evangelistic outreach by that congregation. Perhaps the most widely recognized barrier often is summarized by the term *social class,* but a more accurate description would be to identify it as a liturgical-ethnic-nationality-language-cultural-socioeconomic barrier. A simple illustration of this is that for more than a century, it was very difficult for a Swedish Lutheran congregation in Minnesota or Iowa to reach the Norwegian Lutheran newcomers to that community. Likewise, today it is difficult for a highly liturgical congregation to reach people who seek a more experiential expression of their Christian faith.

The list of barriers to the evangelistic outreach of a congregation is far longer and more complex than most members realize. Unless their existence is recognized, it is highly unlikely that any congregation will attempt to eliminate these barriers; and unless they are identified and eliminated, these barriers will inhibit the evangelistic outreach of the parish.

Unquestionably, the most important of these barriers is within each member. Is the nature of each member's Christian commitment such that it causes him or her to enthusiastically share that faith with others? Or is the commitment to that church one that tends to build a wall around that congregation?

When asked, What is the primary reason you are a member of *this* congregation? the vast majority of adult members of churches offer a reason that refers to a personal contact with a friend or relative who is or was a member of that congregation. "My parents were members here." "I married into this congregation." "A friend at work invited me." "My neighbor asked me to come with her." "A member of this church called on us when we moved here." These are examples of this pattern. In growing congregations the friendship tie accounts for the vast majority of new members. This friendship route into a congregation functions best when members are so enthusiastic about their own faith and what is happening in their church that they cannot help sharing that enthusiasm with others.

A second important barrier also can be found in the attitude of many members. In too many congregations, whenever a new idea is introduced that would expand the opportunities for participation and involvement it is greeted by a series of reasons that this cannot be done here now. Frequently enough members develop sufficient skill in smothering every such suggestion that eventually no one ventures to offer new suggestions. By contrast the congregations oriented toward outreach, evangelism, and the assimilation of new members tend to count the yes votes rather than the no votes and thus eliminate this barrier.[1] The pattern at St. John's had gradually drifted into emphasizing why new ideas cannot be adopted and why new ministries cannot be implemented.

A third barrier to evangelism is that in most congregations, and in nearly all long-established congregations with more than two or three hundred members, it is far easier to become a member than it is to be accepted into the fellowship circle where one feels a part of the fellowship. The membership circle is that large circle which embraces all persons on the membership roll, but the smaller and more intimate fellowship circle includes only those who are accepted and feel a part of this congregation. The larger the congregation and/or the longer it has been in existence, the more difficult it is for new members to climb over that wall surrounding the fellowship circle.

---

[1] For an explanation of how a congregation can focus on counting the yes votes rather than be stalled by the traditional emphasis on counting the no votes, see Lyle E. Schaller and Charles A. Tidwell, *Creative Church Administration* (Nashville: Abingdon, 1975), pp. 38-44.

Where there is a strong family emphasis, and where one-half of today's confirmed members have been there for at least fifteen to twenty years, it often is very difficult for the newcomer to feel a part of such a large and geographically scattered congregation unless the newcomer has either (a) kinfolk in the congregation and/or (b) a very high level of competence in building relationships with strangers. In recent years when relatively few new members had been received, St. John's had gradually become a difficult place to feel at home for the newcomer who was out of practice in building relationships with strangers. One potential response to this barrier is to create new fellowship circles, but this had not been done at St. John's for several years.

A fourth barrier that many congregations build around themselves can be described as the line between the "pioneers" and the "homesteaders." At St. John's the pioneers were those members who had firsthand recollections of the early days of this congregation when it had met in a school as the temporary meeting place in the 1953–1956 era or who remembered "how it was" before the second unit of the building had been completed. The homesteaders were the people who had joined more recently and who did not have firsthand recollections of those early days in the school and in that crowded first unit. Most of the current members also had joined after that first pastor had moved on to another parish. One of the men, who had joined St. John's in 1972 during the tenure of the third pastor, explained the division in these terms: "The pioneers sit around the campfire at every church meeting telling lies about the past to make us homesteaders feel like aliens in a strange land."

In other congregations the line between the pioneers and the homesteaders has been drawn when the congregation moved to a new building at a new location or when a new minister followed the pastor who retired after three decades of service to that same congregation or when a fire destroyed most of the building or when a flood filled the basement and first floor with water, mud, and dead fish or when the key lay leader died or moved away. Every once in awhile an event occurs that advances this dividing line several years and members who had been homesteaders for perhaps as long as a decade or two are "promoted" and accepted as pioneers.

This division between the pioneers and the homesteaders is real in many, many congregations, and it may be helpful to lift up a few facets of this division and suggest why each one is important in understanding how a congregation gradually becomes increasingly exclusive as it unintentionally builds the barriers that keep out prospective new members.

1. Perhaps the most common expression of this division can be found in the nominating committee. Frequently the nominating committee is composed largely of the old pioneers, who tend to nominate other pioneers for office. One reason for this is that church members tend to know by name the people who joined before they joined but are slower in putting together the names and faces of people who join after them. This means the pioneers know most of the other pioneers by name but know a smaller proportion of the homesteaders by name. The larger the proportion of recent new members on the nominating committee, the more likely that a larger number of homesteaders will be nominated for office.

2. The most serious implication of this concept is (a) pioneers normally and naturally expect the newcomers to accept, adopt, and perpetuate the customs, traditions, and value system installed by the pioneers, (b) homesteaders normally and naturally reject many of the customs, traditions, and values that were developed by the pioneers, and (c) the tensions produced by this conflict tend to make either the pioneers or the homesteaders feel rejected.

3. In many congregations in which most of the active members have passed their fiftieth birthday there is a widely shared desire that "we need to bring in more young families, or this congregation will disappear before long." When translated,

this means the pioneers are looking for a new generation of young pioneers to come in and preserve the institution dear to the hearts of the pioneers. This is *not* the agenda the homesteaders bring with them when they seek out a new church home. They are looking for a congregation that will be responsive to their needs, not to help perpetuate someone else's church. This is one of the most effective means of becoming an exclusive church!

4. The larger the congregation and the longer it has been in existence, the more likely it is that (a) the pioneer-homesteader division is real; (b) the pioneers will be seen as an exclusive group by some potential homesteaders; (c) there will be few entry points, in proportion to the size of the congregation, for homesteaders to begin to feel they are a part of the inner core, or fellowship circle; (d) the homesteaders will be asked to be "workers" (Sunday school teachers, callers, ushers, etc.), while the policy-making decisions will be largely reserved for pioneers; and (e) if the pastor is approximately the same age as the pioneers and substantially older than the homesteaders, he will unintentionally reinforce this division.

5. In every long-established congregation the newly arrived pastor automatically is a homesteader (unless he was reared in that congregation or had been a member there before). If he is substantially younger than his predecessor and if his predecessor was seen as an ally of the older pioneers, there is a strong probability that this new, younger pastor will feel more at home with the newer and younger members and that within a few years many of the older pioneers in leadership positions will find themselves being succeeded in office by younger persons. A not uncommon product of this process is the creation of a great number of older ex-leaders who are not happy with "how this church is being run now." After three years at St. John's, Don Johnson suddenly realized one day that he was still seen as a homesteader by a large number of the longtime members.

6. The more obvious the pioneer-homesteader division, the more important that intentional efforts be made to affirm pluralism and, whenever possible, to offer a range of choices in program and schedule to the members. Questions should be phrased in both-and rather than either-or terms.

A fifth congregational barrier that is universal and varies only in degree can be seen in the signs (see chapter 5) that congregations place around themselves. The keep-out signs posted around St. John's, which Don had discussed with the trustees (see pages 100-103), constituted a major barrier to growth for this congregation as it looked toward the second twenty years of its history. Like many other congregations founded before 1970, St. John's had begun to convey the impression that "the only people we expect here are those who have been here at least once before and already know their way around."

A sixth barrier to church growth can be found in the phrase, *When you know you're needed, you know you belong.* The traditional reliance on the pastor and a core of loyal old-timers at St. John's had reduced the chances that a new member or a potential new member would feel needed. The comparatively large size of this congregation and the reliance on longtime members as leaders enhanced this factor. A competent temporary part-time staff member in leadership development could have made a major contribution to the evangelistic outreach of St. John's if that person had been employed in that role back in the 1966–68 period when St. John's was still growing and before it had hit a plateau in its growth pattern.

Perhaps the most subtle of the factors on this list of seven barriers to church growth is the distinction between verbal skills and creative nonverbal skills. St. John's had scores of active members with a very high level of competence in verbal skills. This factor was exacerbated by Don's predecessor, who was (a) exceptionally competent in verbal skills and (b) absolutely opposed to church dinners, bazaars, work days, and other events that offered people the opportunity to express their commitment to Jesus Christ as Lord and Savior by the exercise of their nonverbal creative skills on behalf of the life, ministry, and fellowship of the church. The combination of these factors tended to make the people who did not have that level of competence (and self-confidence) in verbal skills feel unwelcome or out of place. This can be overcome—but it had yet to happen at St. John's—by offering a variety of opportunities in the group life of the parish for people to express themselves through nonverbal creative skills. Examples of this are a quilting circle, an orchestra, a church dinner, a bazaar, an adult group that specializes in doing things or in service projects rather than in study. In order to accommodate existing members and also to have a place for newcomers, there should be at least one such group, class, or circle, for every sixty to ninety participating members. Fewer than that usually means (a) a disproportionately large number of inactive members and (b) comparatively few places for new members to gain a sense of belonging.

While far from complete, this list of seven barriers to church growth does illustrate how the people at St. John's had more control than they realized over the potential growth of this congregation in the years ahead. By what the members decided to do or not to do, this congregation would either remove or reinforce each one of these barriers to church growth. By their actions and inactions the members at St. John's would decide whether this church would cut back or expand its outreach to people who are not a part of any worshiping congregation.

10

LOOKING AT YOUTH MINISTRIES

A few months after he had arrived at St. John's, Don Johnson was meeting one evening with two dozen high-school-age members of the congregation to talk with them about what they would like to see as the components in a package that could be called "ministry to youth." During the course of this discussion he asked them to think of someone employed at their high school whom they trusted, who they felt was a person they could talk with about their problems, who would sympathetically understand their concerns, and who had excellent rapport with high-school students.

"Does everyone here have a picture in your mind of someone who fits this description?" asked Don. "This may be a teacher, counselor, coach, custodian, administrator, or anyone else on the school payroll." When everyone nodded affirmatively, Don added, "Now, tell me approximately how old this person is. You may have to guess, but guess as accurately as you can." After a minute or two of silence broken by some hurried whispered conversations as several sought the help of friends in estimating the ages of the persons involved, the guesses began to flow: forty-four, about fifty, thirty-eight, twenty-nine, thirty-three, about fifty-five, twenty-six, thirty-eight, forty-five, thirty-five, thirty, forty-two, thirty-three, about forty, nearly sixty, thirty-one, thirty-seven, forty-eight, thirty-seven, thirty-five, about thirty-six or thirty-seven, about forty-three or forty-four, I don't know, fifty-five, and about forty-five.

"Let's see," said Pastor Johnson, studying his notes. "Eleven of you named persons in their thirties, eight in their forties, two in their twenties, and three named someone fifty or

144

above. Now what does this say? Most of you named people in their thirties or forties.''

"It simply says that high-school kids relate better to teachers and others in their thirties and forties than to any other age group,'' replied a girl who was one of the natural leaders of the youth group.

"That's because most of the teachers are in their thirties or forties,'' explained a red-haired boy.

"Oh, no! That's not true!'' exclaimed a tall, slender, black-haired girl. "At least one-third of our teachers are under thirty, and it may be closer to half.''

"Yeah, but you can't count most of those. They're too young, and some of them are trying too hard to relate to the kids to pull it off, and the rest act more like big brothers and big sisters than adults,'' explained a seventeen-year-old boy with glasses. "Pastor Johnson asked who it was we relate to best, whom we have good rapport with, who understands our point of view, whom we would choose to go talk to about a problem—and that wipes out most of the teachers who are just out of college. They're not really mature yet themselves. If I want to go to an adult about a problem, I'll go to someone who is in his thirties or forties or older, not someone who is just a little older than I am.''

"There's another factor at work here,'' added a studious-looking blonde girl. "Some teachers like kids, and some don't. Those who don't, tend to get out of teaching by the time they're thirty, and those who do like kids tend to stay in teaching; so when you ask a question like that, naturally you'll get a disproportionately large number of teachers named who are in their thirties or older.''

"You've been very helpful,'' commented Pastor Johnson. "Now let me ask two more follow-up questions. First, when a church goes out to hire someone as youth minister or youth director, what age person do they usually pick?''

"Someone in their twenties," replied eight or ten almost at once.

"Why?" asked Don.

"Because the adults think a young minister can relate to kids." "Because they want someone to be a playmate for the youth." "Because it's cheaper to hire a young adult." "It's the adults and not the youth who do the hiring," came the rush of responses as several of the youth vied for the floor. "No one else will take the job." "The adults don't understand youth, and they think someone else who was in high school more recently will remember how it was to be a teen-ager." "Yeah, but the twenty-six-year-old of today was a teen-ager in a different world from the one we live in today!"

Don Johnson had two reasons for asking these questions of the high-school youth at St. John's. Several months earlier he had heard a speaker comment that he had asked high-school youth from scores of churches this pair of questions concerning the identity and age of a high-school employer with whom they felt good rapport. Of the 1,017 high-school youth who responded, 12 percent named someone age fifty or over, 77 percent named someone in his thirties or forties, and only 11 percent named someone in his twenties. This speaker added that high-school youth tended to estimate the age of adults on the high side, but this factor probably would reduce the proportion age fifty and above by only a few percentage points and increase the proportion in their twenties only slightly. After taking this factor into account it still meant that three-quarters of the youth apparently felt the greatest rapport in youth-adult relationships with someone in the 30–50 age bracket. This did not match Don's impressions, which were based in part on the fact that the vast majority of youth ministers and youth directors he had known were under thirty years of age. Therefore he decided to try the questions on the youth at St. John's. Needless to say, Don was surprised when exactly three-fourths of those responding named someone they believed to be in the 30–50 age group. Therefore Don pursued the issue with the additional questions.

The Future of the Church?

The second reason Don raised this series of questions was that during the weeks following his arrival at St. John's he had begun to feel strong pressures to make a ministry to youth his top priority.

"In my opinion our top priority here at St. John's should be our youth ministry," urged a key member of the church council. "After all, the youth of today are the future leaders of this congregation. If we don't reach the young people today, this congregation will disappear in another twenty years!"

"One of the reasons I was delighted to hear you were going to be our next pastor," added a young mother as she looked at Don, "was that we had been told you were able to relate to youth. I believe a major reason for our recent decline in membership has been that we have not been able to reach and hold our youth."

"How can anyone expect this church to continue to grow when most of our youth move away as soon as they finish high school? If we could keep our young people, our future could be brighter," declared a fifty-seven-year-old member of St. John's who had been a charter member. "There's nothing for them to do here; there just aren't many jobs here. I can understand why they move away, but it breaks my heart to see them leave," she continued. "Every time I see or hear of one of our young people moving away, I think, 'That's one less member for the St. John's of tomorrow.' "

Do any of these comments sound familiar? If they do, it might be helpful to look at several dimensions of this concept that "the future of this church depends on our ability to reach the youth of today." It was an issue that dominated the agenda for much of Don Johnson's pastorate at St. John's.

Not a Growth Concept

While it is normal for the adults at St. John's to hope that the youth of today will be the adult members of that congregation in the years ahead, actual experience suggests this is not the pattern.

First, in nearly all rapidly growing congregations the growth in numbers is composed largely—and often almost entirely—of persons who joined these congregations as adults. In the typical rapidly growing congregation the adult membership consists almost entirely of persons who are first-generation members of *that* congregation. Adult members who are the children of older members are few in number and constitute a tiny proportion of the total adult membership.

Second, research over a period of years indicates that the urban or suburban congregations in which children of members constitute more than 30 percent of the current adult leadership almost always are congregations that are diminishing in size.

Why?

One piece of speculation suggests that the congregation that chooses its leaders from second- and third-generation members seldom is able to reach and to assimilate into leadership positions adults who have no previous relationships with this congregation. Most of the exceptions to this pattern tend to be found in the smaller denominations such as the Christian Reformed Church, the Reformed Church in America, and the several branches of the Mennonite family of churches.

A Typical Pattern

What is the typical pattern?

How many of those young persons who were members of this congregation when they were seniors in high school are members of the same congregation a decade later?

In urban and suburban churches the typical response is 15 percent. Why? School, indifference, employment opportunities, rebellion against imposed values, and/or marriage have taken the other 85 percent away to other communities or other congregations or out of an active role in any congregation.

In churches in those nonmetropolitan counties which are stable in terms of the number of residents or which are experiencing an increase in population, it is not uncommon to find a congregation in which 30 percent of the high-school seniors of a decade ago are members of that congregation today, but it is unusual to find one in which more than half of the high-school seniors of ten years ago are still active *resident* members of that congregation.

"But What If . . ."

"But what if our young people don't stay with us—what's the future of this congregation?"

From a strictly pragmatic perspective the best response to that frequently heard plea is that the replacement population for most congregations should be seen as other adults who are not active in the life of any worshiping congregation today.

The outstanding examples of this can be seen in scores of healthy, vigorous, vital, mission-minded congregations in (a) those fifteen hundred rural counties in which the population has been declining for decade after decade and (b) older central cities all across the nation. In most of these congregations an analysis of the membership roster reveals that the vast majority of the members under age fifty are persons who united with this congregation as adults and only a minority are persons who grew up in that church.

"But what if we focus our efforts on a ministry to adults and to adults who are not active in any congregation—what will happen to our young people? Are you suggesting we totally neglect our ministry to youth?"

Again the experiences of many congregations suggest that the best response to this question is to see it not as an either-or issue, but rather as a both-and concern. In general, the churches with the best ministry to youth are those congregations which also have an effective ministry to adults in the 25-40 age group (see item 1 on page 151) and which also have the capability to reach *and to assimilate* into the fellowship circle (see "Seven Barriers to Church Growth," chapter 9) adults who have no kinfolk within the membership. Perhaps the one dimension of any effort to minister to youth that deserves special emphasis should be the development of an effective ministry to younger adults *and* the expansion of the capacity of the congregation to reach, accept, affirm, and assimilate persons younger than the parents of the youth of the church.

Means or End?

The most significant dimensions of this issue can be summarized in the word "why." Is the emphasis on making a ministry to youth a top priority motivated by a concern for the salvation of these young people? Is it motivated by a desire to bring the Good News of Jesus Christ to young people? Is it motivated by a concern for the institutional survival of *this* congregation? Is it motivated by a desire to secure more members?

Every institution and organization is vulnerable to the temptation to exploit people on behalf of the institutional needs of that organization. The church is no exception! Whenever the desire to develop a strong youth ministry is motivated by a concern for "the future of our church" there is the risk the result will be exploitation.

The Good News

For the benefit and reassurance of those who have read this far with a mixture of doubts, questions, negative feelings, and perhaps even some hostility, there is some good news. The future of the church is not in the hands of the youth of today, it is in God's hands! He is at work in the world today, and he will judge us and our efforts not on the basis of whether or not we have been able to keep our young people within this congregation, but on the basis of faithfulness and obedience.

A Checklist for Looking at Youth Ministries

Many congregations have developed a specialized ministry to older adults. A few have developed a very important and redemptive ministry to single parents. A very large number of congregations are working hard to improve their ministry to young married couples with small children. Several have developed an excellent specialized ministry to single young adults. A few others are specializing in a ministry to college students. Nearly every Protestant congregation, however, wants to build an excellent ministry to high-school-age youth. Some have achieved this goal, but in many congregations the discussions on this subject consists of a mixture of hope, frustration, concern about institutional survival, scapegoating, nostalgia, and envy. A more constructive approach is to review some of the characteristics that keep reappearing among those congregations which have a strong ministry to youth. In reviewing this list it should be emphasized that it is very unusual for every one of these characteristics to be found in the youth ministry of a single congregation, but most churches with an excellent youth program merit a grade of A or A- on at least six or seven of the items on this list.

1. Perhaps the one item on this list that arouses the least general attention is that most congregations with a good youth ministry also have an effective ministry to adults under age 40. While it is impossible to prove a cause-and-effect relationship, this coincidence appears too often to be ignored. The other side of this picture is that it is rare for the congregation in which there

are few adults in the 35–40 age bracket to have an excellent youth program. The relationship clearly is *not* simply that some of the parents of high-school youth are in the 35–40 age group. It may be that those churches which provide a meaningful ministry to adults in the 25–40 age range are best equipped to be relevant to the needs of youth. It may be that the volunteer lay counselors for youth groups often come out of this age group. It may be that the best beginning point in developing a strong youth ministry is first to develop a meaningful ministry to adults under 40. What do you think?

2. The easiest method of organizing people into a cohesive group with common interests, common goals, and a sense of unity is to identify an "enemy" and organize against this enemy. This is a tactic that is widely used in organizing election campaigns, community organizations, labor unions, and reform movements. Occasionally it is used in organizing a youth fellowship in the church. The most frequently identified enemies are, in this order of frequency, (a) parents, (b) the schools, (c) the church, and (d) the senior minister. Since the Christian church is founded on love and forgiveness, this organizational tactic should never be used in any ministry of the church.

3. The best youth ministries are based on an agenda that begins with the needs, the concerns, the questions, the problems, and the dreams of the youth. The old model of organizing a youth fellowship in order to (a) have a good youth fellowship, (b) round out a complete program package for all ages, (c) satisfy parents and older adults, (d) keep the kids out of trouble, (e) hopefully cause youth to want to grow up to be like older adults, and (f) "teach the kids the Bible" is less and less effective. The lesson that was discovered by the foreign missionary movement several decades ago is now being rediscovered in developing youth ministries. In order to talk to people about Jesus Christ it is necessary first to listen to their concerns and needs. (Luke 8:24-56; Luke 10:29–11:14.)

4. Increasingly, youth programs are emphasizing active and

experiential learning opportunities rather than passive educational programs. Frequently these are combined with opportunities for Christian service and witness. Examples of this experiential approach include the work-camp trip to a poverty area, the youth-music combination that provides the opportunity for youth to witness to their faith through music, the community service project using an action-reflection educational model, and the walk-for-hunger event.

5. The churches with the best youth programs minister to the adult lay volunteer counselors. The worst youth programs use adult volunteers and discard them when they are burned out. The best youth programs are in churches where there is an intentional and systematic effort to identify, recruit, train, place, and support lay volunteers for their role as counselors. This effort includes regular lay training events for counselors (usually in cooperation with other congregations), at least a half hour for debriefing and reflection after each meeting of the youth fellowship, development of a meaningful support group of and for these lay volunteers, and a church-wide recognition that this is an important ministry.

6. The best youth programs do not attempt to include all youth of the same age bracket in one group. In these ministries there is an awareness of (a) the vast differences among youth of the same chronological age, (b) the differences across age groupings, and (c) the fact that persons born since 1950 have been trained for their entire life to assume that society offers high-school youth a wide range of choices. Sometimes one congregation will intentionally attempt to reach one or two groups within one age bracket on Sunday morning through a youth choir and/or a Sunday school class, and overlapping but not identical group through an evening program. In smaller congregations, where there are relatively few youth in one age category, a similar goal is achieved by two or three or four or five congregations working together and offering alternative programs. The key to this approach is that adults not be anxious

that every high-school-age young person participate in *every* program for youth offered in *our* church.

7. The congregations with the best youth ministries usually have progressed beyond the token youth representative on the governing board of the church and now seek to discover where the young people feel they can serve most effectively, rather than establish a youth quota for each board and committee or, worse, have a youth board composed entirely of adults who plan for youth without the participation of youth!

8. Many of the congregations with excellent ministries to youth have recognized that peer-group relationships and adult models are very influential in the development of the value systems, habits, and attitudes among high-school youth. In these congregations these factors are very important in the selection of youth counselors in planning the organizational structure of the package of programs that constitutes the youth ministry and in guiding program planning.

9. Some of the best youth ministries are built around a combination of ministry to youth and music or a combination youth-music-drama focus with an intentional effort to provide a meaningful place for each person, regardless of musical, vocal, or dramatic talents.

10. A very common characterisitc of the best youth ministries is the use of short-term events, experiences, trips, weekend retreats, social occasions, service projects, and meaningful tasks in strengthening the ties that bind individuals into the group. In some congregations this is reinforced with a covenant agreement developed by members of the group which often becomes the most important factor in making a group out of a collection of individuals.

What if your congregation scores a grade of A or A- on every one of these ten items? This is not a guarantee that you will have an excellent youth ministry, but it certainly does provide what appears to be the context for excellence.

11

EVALUATING THE GOAL-SETTING PROCESS

"Any objections if I put up this sign?" asked Pastor Don Johnson of Chet McKinney. They were preparing for a congregational meeting at which the planning committee, chaired by Chet McKinney, would present its first report.

The Reverend Mr. Donald Johnson is basically a strongly goal-oriented individual, and when he had arrived at St. John's nearly two years earlier he found a congregation that appeared to be drifting along on a downward curve after a fifteen-year period of comparatively rapid growth in the 1950s and 1960s. One of his first efforts had been to build support for a planning committee, which eventually was appointed and assigned the responsibility to recommend some specific goals for St. John's for the coming year.

"What does it say?" asked Chet as he came over to see the hand-lettered sign Don was carrying. On a 22-x-28-inch sheet of cardboard Pastor Johnson had copied this quotation from the booklet *Trustees As Servants*, written by Robert K. Greenleaf:

The first thing an institution needs to do to start on a conspicuously higher course is to state clearly where it wants to go, whom it wants to serve, and how it expects those served directly as well as society at large, to benefit from the service. Unless these are clearly stated, an institution cannot approach its optimum performance. Yet the internal administrators, left to themselves, usually hesitate to state goals so precisely.

"That's great!" responded Chet McKinney as he read the sign. "Put it on the wall right above where our committee will be sitting, so everyone can see it while we make and discuss our report.''

A half hour later the meeting at which the planning committee of St. John's would make its first report was opened with prayer by Pastor Johnson. He began this devotional period by reading from Matthew 7:24-27.

"These are the first of a series of goals we are suggesting for this congregation for the coming year," explained Chet McKinney to the gathering of nearly sixty members that Tuesday evening. "We expect to add another twelve to fourteen to the list, but we didn't want to wait until we had completed the full list before receiving your comments, ideas, suggestions, criticisms, objections, and insights. We think the best way we can explain the goal-setting process we are launching here at St. John's is to bring a sample of our work to you and seek your reactions." As he spoke, Chet pointed to a sheet of newsprint on the wall to his right on which were listed these six goals. "What do you think of these for openers?" he asked.

1. We plan to do more for our older members.
2. We plan to receive thirty new adult members by letter of transfer or by profession of faith.
3. We plan to strengthen our ministry to youth.
4. We plan to have each Sunday school teacher attend at least one workshop or lab school on Christian education.
5. We plan to raise $1,000 in second-mile giving next year by the members toward the relief of world hunger.
6. By September 1 next year we will paint and refurbish two Sunday school rooms at an estimated cost of $1,600.

It may be helpful to the reader, as well as to the planning committee at St. John's, to analyze the firstfruits of the goal-setting process and to seek to discover how that process might be improved. This can be accomplished by measuring these goals against seven separate guidelines that can be used by every congregation as it engages in a goal-setting effort.

SAM

The first and third goals on this list raise the question that often is described by the acronym SAM. SAM stands for specific, attainable, and measurable. By the definition used here, a goal is something that you can tell when you have reached—"I should like to be in my garden at home by 5:00 P.M. today" is a simple example of this. The first and third items on this list actually are hopes or dreams or wishes. Frequently that is a beginning point in the goal-setting process, but the wishes and hopes must be translated into specific, attainable, and measurable terms.

Under the first item on the list, the people at St. John's might decide to (a) tape the worship service every Sunday and make sure this tape is made available to every shut-in at least twice a month, (b) plan a twelve-day trip to visit a mission church in Brazil with at least five older (past age fifty-five) persons going on that trip next year, (d) develop two new avenues by which older members can express their Christian commitment by being involved in ministry to others, or (d) by September 15 organize a new Sunday school class for older widowed women not now in any adult Sunday school class.

In regard to youth, St. John's might translate that goal into (a) electing at least two persons under age twenty to the governing board; (b) making the church building available on Tuesday nights during the school year as a place where youth can come to meet friends, study, talk, play games, or watch television; or (c) by September 1 identify, recruit, provide training opportunities for, and invite to be youth counselors six adult members who have not been active in the youth program.

In each case it should be possible to determine by the end of next year whether each goal has been attained. This cannot be accomplished unless each goal is stated in more specific terms. How will anyone be able to tell fourteen months from now whether or not St. John's is "doing more for the older members" or that it has "strengthened the ministry to youth"?

Control

Perhaps the most common pitfall in the goal-setting process is the temptation to set goals in areas over which those setting the goals do not have control. This is illustrated here by items two and four. The goal to receive thirty new adult members is poorly worded. The people at St. John's do not have control over whether people decide to unite with that congregation. All God asks of each of us is to be faithful and obedient. All St. John's has control over is what the members do or do not do.

Five better ways to state the wish that is behind that second goal might be: (a) during the next year we will invite at least one hundred adults to join this congregation; (b) during the next year we will make five hundred visitation-evangelism calls on people who are not now actively involved in the life of any congregation; (c) within six months we will organize a "fisherman's club" with at least eight members, and each member will spend at least one evening or afternoon every week in visitation-evangelism; (d) by the end of next year we will have identified at least six of the barriers (see pages 137 to 143) that, without knowing that we were doing it, we have built around this congregation and that tend to discourage prospective new members from becoming interested in this congregation; or (e) by September 30 next year we will have had at least one lay witness mission here that will strengthen the faith and enhance the ability of at least twenty of our members to witness to their Christian commitment to others.

Direction

The third guideline that can be used in evaluating these six goals is found in the quotation from Robert K. Greenleaf that

Pastor Johnson had posted on the wall at St. John's. The planning committee clearly is anxious to get things moving again, but no direction has been stated. Which way do we want to go? The sixty people gathered that Tuesday evening had no idea of the direction that the planning committee was intending to go; therefore it was impossible for them to decide whether (a) they agreed with that direction (purpose) or (b) the goals being suggested were consistent with that direction.

One of the basic reasons that every congregation needs some generalized statement of purpose or direction is to guide the goal-setting process, whether that process be a formal or a highly informal one. The second basic value of a statement of purpose is as a benchmark for evaluating specific goals as they are formulated.

This problem can be described in more specific language by looking at these six goals being discussed at St. John's. A quick reading of the six suggests that the top priority at St. John's is enchancing the ministry to older adults. Or is the top priority a ministry to youth? Or a growth in size? Or strengthening the Christian education program? Or the spiritual, personal, and professional growth of the teachers? Or world hunger? Or improving the appearance of the interior of the building?

Which is the end, or central, purpose? Which are the means to the end? What are the priorities at St. John's? How do these goals express those priorities? How do these goals help the members understand and affirm those priorities?

Benefits

A fourth guideline for analyzing and strengthening the goal-setting process also can be found in that quotation from Greenleaf. How will the people being served by St. John's benefit from these goals? The point of this question can be seen more clearly by looking at the first four goals on the list. How will the older members benefit from an effort to "do more" for them? Will they feel more dependent on St. John's? Will their spiritual life be enriched? Will they be less lonely? Or will some feel more harried? Will they feel more exhausted?

How will any prospective new members benefit from uniting with St. John's? What is it that St. John's has to offer them that will cause them to be glad they united with that congregation? Would they be better served by joining some other congregation in the community? Or is St. John's more interested in reversing the downward curve of its growth line over the past several years than it is in trying to define how anyone would benefit by joining this church?

Is the effort to strengthen the youth ministry motivated by a desire ''to keep our young people in the church'' (see chapter 10) or to be more responsive to their needs? Which is the more important benefit behind this goal, the future of the youth or the future of St. John's?

Is the fourth goal, involving Sunday school teachers in workshops and lab schools, motivated by a concern for the teachers or by a concern over the diminishing size of the Sunday school at St. John's?

In simple terms, this issue of benefits forces the people involved in setting goals to struggle with such questions as: Who is the client? Who is the intended beneficiary of this goal? and Who do we expect will receive the primary benefits of the effort to implement this goal? This comes through very clearly in the second, third, and fourth goals on the list at St. John's. Who is the client? Potential new members at St. John's? The young people or St. John's? The Sunday school teachers or St. John's? Who is expected to be the beneficiary of each goal?

Ownership

The fourth goal on this list calls for more in-service training for Sunday school teachers. This is an admirable wish, but it again raises the question of control. In addition, it raises the question of ownership. By definition, a good goal is one that *I* have had a part in formulating. A bad goal is one that *someone else* developed and wants me to implement. Since all of St. John's Sunday school teachers are Christians, they naturally will not choose to implement bad goals! In other words, who "owns" the idea that every Sunday school teacher should be involved in a continuing education program? The teachers? Or the planning committee? There is an old saying in adult education that "you cannot teach an adult anything he or she does not want to learn." Unless each teacher feels that he or she owns a part of this goal, it is a bad goal.

This fourth goal also reflects the question of control. The planning committee lost control of the implementation process when the goal was stated in these words. The control has now passed to the people (unidentified) who will make the workshops and lab schools available and the teachers who may or may not attend.

In addition, the question of resources was ignored in formulating this goal. Who will provide the resources necessary to implement this goal?

A better way to have stated this goal might have been: (a) St. John's will budget $400 to enable three to seven Sunday school teachers to attend a workshop or lab school during the coming year, (b) this congregation will pay the tuition or registration, meals, housing, and one-half of the transportation costs with a maximum of seventy-five dollars per teacher to enable two to eight teachers to attend a workshop or lab school next year, (c) this congregation will sponsor a Friday-night and all-day-Saturday overnight retreat and workshop for Sunday school teachers before the end of next year, or (d) if our cluster of churches goes ahead with the current proposal to provide two training events a year for Sunday school teachers, we will pay all expenses of the teachers who participate in either or both events.

At this point in the discussion of their initial report, one of the members of the planning committee at St. John's commented:

"I guess I see what you mean by SAM, by the need for an umbrella statement of purpose, by the need to be sure we agree who the client is, by ownership and control; and I agree we should sharpen up the wording of those first four goals. Now what do you have to say about the one goal of raising $1,000 for world hunger? Doesn't that meet all the requirements of a good goal?"

A response to that question requires moving on to the sixth in this series of seven guidelines for evaluating the goal-setting process in a church.

Balance

Both of the last two goals on this list are specific, attainable, and measurable. The implementation of both is clearly within the control of the members at St. John's, and presumably there is local ownership or these two goals would not be on the list.

In evaluating the quality of these two goals, however, another pitfall merits discussion. This is the question of balance; do the goals of the congregation reflect a balanced definition of purpose? Too often the goals are stated in terms that encourage people to choose up sides on a specific goal. If the goal is implemented, some people will feel alienated since they lost. If the goal is not implemented, a different group of members will feel like losers and alienated from the congregation.

Many congregations have had good experiences in developing three categories of specific goals under the more general goal of second-mile giving. This concept can be illustrated by looking at the last two of the six goals in this list at St. John's. It might be helpful to have goals five and six stated in this form.

5. Encourage second-mile giving to various causes.
   a. $1,000 for world hunger.
   b. $1,600 for renovating two Sunday school rooms.
   c. $400 for the training of additional lay volunteers as youth counselors.

While these three goals have the common characteristic of being financed by second-mile, designated giving, they cover three different dimensions of the purpose of the church. One goal is outreach, a second is housekeeping, and the third reflects program. Members who oppose one or two of these can vote in favor of the general goal by designating their second-mile giving for the one they do approve.

Some congregations build this concept into general program-planning efforts every year, and typically the combined receipts for the three second-mile giving ventures will be equal to 10 to 15 percent of the regular budget. In what is now the longest continuous inflationary era in American history this approach has enabled many congregations to finance goals that were squeezed out of the regular budget-building process. In looking at this concept, the important point to remember is the emphasis on reflecting a balanced definition of purpose including both outreach and ministry to people as well as the more easily defined housekeeping goals.

Reporting

Perhaps the major fringe benefit of the goal-setting process is that the list of goals offers a useful outline as the leaders plan to report to the members on the life and ministry of this congregation during the past year. The failure to take advantage of this fringe benefit is one of the most common pitfalls in goal-setting and implementation. Conspicuously missing from the presentation at St. John's was any system for reporting to the members later on the progress made in attaining these goals. The reporting on goals often can be combined with the presentation of the "Silver Beavers" (see chapter 4) through a series of slides, movies, and skits.

Three examples of how this has been done will illustrate the concept. In one church there is a special worship service every January in which the congregation gives thanks to God for (a) the opportunities and challenges they were confronted with during the past year and (b) the resources they have been given with which to respond to these opportunities and challenges. The list of goals of the past year and the progress made in achieving each one constitute a major part of the "outline" for this special worship service. When they leave this special worship service the members go home feeling they are a part of a parish where things are happening. This gives visibility to many goals that do not have a naturally high level of visibility.

In another congregation the list of eighteen to twenty annual goals is printed on the back of the bulletin cover, and once a month four or five members get together for a "bulletin party" and indicate with a colored felt-tip pen the progress that has been made in accomplishing each goal. These bulletin covers are used the following Sunday; and the people present receive, on the back of that Sunday's bulletin, an up-to-date report on the goal implementation process.

A third approach is used at the annual meeting of one congregation that uses the list of goals for the past year as the heart of the reporting process on the year just ended. The goals for the coming year are described as a part of the look-to-the-future emphasis in the second half of what is usually a very interesting three-hour annual meeting. The distinctive feature of the first half of this annual meeting is the use of color slides and a tape cassette in describing the past year in review. Within a week the slides and tape cassette will have been taken to every shut-in, so each can see and hear this summary of what happened during the past twelve months.

Before moving on to another chapter in the life of St. John's Church and the career of Pastor Don Johnson, it may be helpful to raise a larger and more basic question about this planning effort at St. John's.

At St. John's the planning committee saw itself charged with the responsibility of setting goals or doing the planning for this parish. This is a very widespread practice. Planning committees usually are expected to plan.

A different approach, which has both advantages and disadvantages, is to ask the planning committee to cause planning to happen. In this approach a special committee encourages every program and administrative committee to plan; and this special committee encourages, monitors, prods, facilitates, coordinates, and examines all these separate planning efforts. The special committee does very little planning, but it asks many questions of those who are doing the planning. How does this relate to the overall purpose of this congregation? Where will the resources come from for this? How do your goals fit into the goals of this other program department? When do you expect to achieve that goal? What will be some of the implications for others if you do attain it? What will be some of the implications for others if you do not attain it? How does that goal relate to what has been set as the top congregation-wide priorities for the coming year? Who is the client for this goal? Who will benefit from that program? Do the people you are planning for feel a sense of ownership of that goal? Is that the way you want to state that goal? What is your timeline? Who will have to approve that goal before it can be implemented?

At St. John's the planning committee saw its role as goal-setting. Who should ask these questions at St. John's? Who asks them in your congregation?

12

DON'T BE THE FIRST ASSOCIATE!
BE THE THIRD

"A friend of mine and I would like to come over and spend an hour or two with you," explained the Reverend Kenneth McCall to Don Johnson over the telephone one sunny April morning in the third year of Don's pastorate at St. John's Church. After a minute or two of small talk they agreed that lunch a week from next Thursday would be a convenient time.

As he replaced the telephone receiver Don mused: "I wonder what he has on his mind? Ken and I have known each other for at least a dozen years, but I don't consider him a close friend by any means. Why is he willing to make a three hundred and twenty mile round-trip drive and kill a day just to have lunch with me? Maybe he has a problem at Hope Church that he thinks I can help him with, but I doubt if I can be of any help to him."

At the other end of that conversation Ken McCall cradled the telephone in its holder and smiled across the desk at his close friend Bill Schroeder. "The more I think about it, Bill, the more I'm convinced Don's the man we're looking for. I hate to ask you to take a whole day off from work, but it's very important that we have your opinion before we pursue this beyond a get-acquainted luncheon."

"No problem, Ken. I'm glad we could agree on a day when I can go along with you. This is very important! After one unfortunate experience with an inexperienced associate minister, it is essential we pick a winner this time."

Bill Schroeder is not only a close friend of Pastor McCall, he also is one of the most influential leaders at Hope Church and one of the handful of charter members remaining from that

October 1958 Sunday evening when a score of people had gathered to discuss forming a new congregation on the growing northern edge of a city with nearly 150,000 residents. Bill and his wife, Agnes, were young parents in the late 1950s, and they were very enthusiastic about the possibility of launching a new congregation near where they had purchased their home. During the next two decades Bill and Agnes doubled the number of their children to four; moved another two miles farther out to a larger home; and bade a very sad farewell to their close friend, the Reverend John Walker, who had served as the founding pastor of Hope Church and had moved on at the end of ten years. When Walker left, attendance at Sunday morning worship averaged 360, and rarely were there fewer than 300 in Sunday school. He was followed by Roger Burke, who stayed slightly over two years and who left behind a congregation averaging 265 at worship and a fading hope of the permanent sanctuary that was to complete the original three-stage master plan prepared in 1959.

The first two units of that master plan had been constructed during Walker's ten-year pastorate. The first unit, the fellowship hall, which was to serve as a temporary sanctuary, was ready for occupancy in late 1960. This unit also included four classrooms, a small suite of offices, and a kitchen. The second unit, a twelve-room educational wing, was completed in 1966, just as the nation began what turned out to be the longest inflationary era in American history. Bill Schroeder had headed the group that spearheaded the drive to build this second unit, despite the opposition of many members who were convinced they should finish paying off the mortgage on the fellowship hall before starting a second building program. During the next decade Bill derived considerable satisfaction from this experience as he watched the congregation use increasingly cheap dollars to pay back the expensive dollars they had borrowed in 1966.

The two-year pastorate of Roger Burke was followed by the don't-rock-the-boat ministry of the gentle Wilbur Lee. Dr. Lee

left after four years to become a college teacher. While Bill
Schroeder liked Dr. Lee as a person and a preacher, he felt that
Lee was not the dynamic leader that Hope needed in the early
1970s. Instead of an imaginative and aggressive person-oriented
leader, as John Walker had been, Lee was a gentle teacher who
preferred books to people. During Lee's fifty-month tenure,
more people left Hope Church than came into membership, the
worship attendance sagged to an average of 225 on Sunday
morning, and the dollar receipts hit a plateau in the $65,000
range. The minister blamed the decline on the fact that the
church was understaffed and he was overworked. At his urging,
the fading hope of building the permanent sanctuary was
replaced by the challenge to add a second minister to the staff.

The forty-three-year-old Ken McCall followed Dr. Lee, and
he immediately impressed Bill Schroeder as exactly the minister
that Hope Church needed. Prior to coming to Hope he had
served two seven-year pastorates in suburban congregations
similar in type to, but somewhat smaller in membership than,
Hope Church. Both had been started in the decade following
World War II. In both these situations congregational morale
was low when McCall arrived. In both he had reversed a
statistical decline in the membership and attendance figures, and
both were vital, vigorous, strong, and evangelistic congregations when he left. He arrived at Hope Church with an
impressive record, a high level of self-esteem and commendable
self-confidence, a very supportive wife, three children, and the
leaders' assurance that as soon as he was ready the members
were prepared to begin the search for an associate minister.

He arrived to find a seventeen-year-old congregation that was
within a year of paying off the mortgage and that was beginning
the seventh year of a continuing decline in size, morale, and
enthusiasm. Worship attendance averaged 225 on Sunday
morning. An attendance survey revealed that during the previous
May, 100 members had attended one Sunday, 63 members had
attended twice, 86 members were present three Sundays, 72

members had been at worship all four Sundays, and 315 members had not attended even once in May. In other words, 49 percent of the 636 confirmed members had not been present for Sunday morning worship even once during this "average" month of May. On the typical Sunday morning, the worshiping congregation included 193 confirmed members, 24 children not yet confirmed, 5 visitors, and 3 constituents.

As he compared these figures with each of the two previous congregations he had served, Ken was disturbed. In the parish he served immediately before coming to Hope, a typical month saw between 75 and 80 percent of the confirmed membership at worship at least once. In the congregation he served before that, he watched that percentage climb from 53 percent when he arrived to 88 percent by the time he had left. While a part of that change was the product of a very thorough cleaning of the membership rolls, most of it was the result of Ken's dynamic leadership.

As he looked at the figures for Hope he reflected: "Unless there is a lot of dead wood in the membership roll, we should be averaging at least 300 at worship and perhaps 340 to 360. Why are we averaging only 225? Why are so many members staying away? Why did the attendance drop from 360 to 225 in less than seven years?"

Next the newly arrived pastor looked at the median tenure of the current membership. Ken found that one-half of the 736 confirmed members had been members of this seventeen-year-old congregation for at least eleven years, and one-half had joined during the past eleven years. For the typical healthy urban or suburban congregation the median tenure of the current membership usually is between seven and ten years (except at Old First Church downtown, where the unusually strong loyalty ties typically raise this to twelve or thirteen years). In a relatively new congregation such as this one, that median tenure should be seven or eight, not eleven, years. As he studied these statistics, talked with the leaders, and visited in the homes, Pastor McCall concluded that one of the basic reasons for the low participation rate was that many members had been neglected during the exciting days of rapid growth and building construction. The congregation had grown so rapidly and the building program had taken so much of the leaders' time that although new members were received, a large proportion of them were not assimilated into the fellowship of Hope Church.

With the strong support of Bill Schroeder, Pastor McCall pushed vigorously for the authorization to seek a second minister for the staff at Hope Church. When someone asked, "What will this new minister do?" Pastor McCall had an immediate answer. "The question is not what he will do. The issue we're dealing with here is what didn't get done when this congregation was seriously understaffed for several years. Today we're seeing and feeling the results of what didn't get done back then. When a congregation is understaffed, as this one was understaffed back in the 1960s, the impact of what doesn't get done in program development, assimilation of new members, broadening the base of participation, and care of members doesn't begin to be felt for about five years. We're now feeling that impact, and we need to do what was neglected earlier."

Eventually the finance committee agreed that money could be found to hire an assistant minister at minimum salary. To compress a painful experience into a few sentences, Hope Church proceeded to call a promising graduate from an excellent seminary as its first assistant minister. Nineteen months after he arrived, he left. He left feeling disillusioned, unhappy, under-employed, ill-treated, unaccepted, closed out of the leadership circle, frustrated, and unfulfilled. The leaders at Hope, including Ken and Bill, were pleased when he announced that he was leaving to go back to graduate school. They felt that Hope Church had been cheated, that the young assistant had not earned his salary, that he had not displayed the initiative and creativity they had hoped for, and that he had "never learned how to work."

After several months of discussion it was decided, at the urging of Pastor McCall, to change the job title from "assistant minister" to "associate minister," to increase the salary by $4,500, and to seek someone with at least ten years of pastoral experience.

This entire effort had taken nearly three years. By that time the worship attendance at Hope Church had climbed back up to an average of 285, and most of the members agreed that continued growth would require a second pastor on the staff. A few old-timers muttered, "If John Walker could serve this congregation all by himself when we were averaging over 350 at worship, I don't know why we need two ministers now when we're not even averaging 300." Most of the members, however, agreed that this was a far more complex parish than it had been a decade earlier and supported the effort to find an experienced minister to help Ken McCall.

A natural leader, Ken took the major responsibility for seeking an associate minister. With strong support now for finding an experienced pastor for the position, Ken began going over in his mind the names of ministers he knew who were effective pastors. He wanted someone who was younger than himself, in a situation where the salary offered by Hope would be competitive with what that person was now receiving, and who had been in the present pastorate at least a couple of years. He also sought someone who he thought would be creative, a self-starter, personally compatible with himself, and, most of all, someone who apparently enjoyed and gained a sense of fulfillment from serving as a pastor. The name of Don Johnson floated to the top of his list. He first checked his impressions with some of his ministerial friends who also knew Don, and they had nothing but very favorable comments to offer.

After discussing this possibility with his close friend Bill Schroeder and a half dozen other leaders at Hope Church, Ken called Don and arranged the luncheon appointment.

Over lunch Ken and Bill described the situation at Hope

Church to Don. After an hour's conversation Ken and Bill looked at each other, and Bill gave an almost imperceptible affirmative nod of his head. Ken said: "Don, the real reason for our visit with you is not to tell you about what has happened at Hope in the past, but to ask you if you would be interested in coming over and being a part of the future with us at Hope. Are you interested in talking about that?"

Don Johnson was completely surprised by the question. He had wondered why these two men, one an acquaintance and one a complete stranger, had driven so far simply to have lunch with him. Since he did not feel that he could leave St. John's, it had never occurred to him they might be coming over to ask him to join the staff at Hope.

"Sorry, but no, absolutely no," replied Don. "I'm flattered that you thought of me and impressed that you have come so far to see me, but there is no way—absolutely no way—that I can leave St. John's. Now what else do you have on your agenda that we should talk about?"

As they drove back together Ken McCall apologized to his friend: "I'm sorry, Bill, that I caused you to take a whole day off from work for nothing, but I thought we might be able to interest Don in coming over to Hope. I guess we just invested a day on a wild goose chase."

"You don't have to apologize, Ken," responded Bill Schroeder. "This was a very profitable day. I'm very impressed with Pastor Johnson, and I agree that he's the man we're looking for. He passed the first test, so let's talk about what we do next."

"What do you mean, he passed the first test?" inquired a puzzled Pastor McCall.

"Simple. He told us no, he couldn't leave where he is now," came the response. "If he had been eager to explore this further, I would have been concerned that maybe he was primarily interested in leaving where he is now rather than attracted by the possibility of coming to Hope. Now that we know that's not the case he looks very attractive to me. We don't want to call a pastor who is motivated to accept the call because he wants to get out of where he is. We want someone who is happy where he is and thus automatically rejects our first overture.''

A month later the telephone rang, and when Don Johnson answered it, he was greeted by the cheerful voice of Ken McCall. "Good morning, Don. Have you reconsidered your decision and decided to join our team here at Hope Church?"

"No, I'm afraid not," replied Don. "I certainly do appreciate being asked, and I recognize there are great possibilities in ministry for you folks at Hope; but I don't believe the Lord is calling me to join you. I don't believe I've finished my work here at St. John's.''

"We can't agree with you on that, Don," responded Ken. "Bill Scheoeder and I have talked about this with several of our members, and they all agreed that I should call you again. We're convinced God wants us to ask you to bring your many talents and skills and put them to work here. You think about it, talk it over with your wife, pray about it, and I'll call you back in a week. We're convinced the Lord has great things in the future for Hope Church, and we need you to help bring them to reality.''

Before that telephone call Don had almost completely dismissed from his mind the idea of looking into this unexpected possibility of becoming the associate pastor at Hope Church. Now, having been asked twice, what should he do?

Criteria for Deciding

What should Don do? Should he explore this possibility further? Dismiss it completely? What criteria should he use in making that decision? There are at least seven or eight factors that merit consideration when making this type of decision.

Obviously the first is the question of a call. Is this a call from God that he wants Don to move from St. John's to Hope? Is this the best way he can serve the Lord? Or does God want him to remain at St. John's? This is not an easy question to resolve, but clearly it tops the list as Don wrestles with this invitation.

A second factor is that here is a congregation that has (a) prospered with the pastoral leadership of two strong ministers in John Walker and Ken McCall, (b) had a disastrous experience with its first assistant minister, (c) apparently concluded the reason for that unhappy experience was the inexperience of that first assistant minister, (d) decided that the way to eliminate the problem was to seek an experienced associate pastor, and (e) apparently assumed that the entire fault for that first unhappy experience was with the young seminary graduate and that the congregation shared none of the blame for that disaster.

A more realistic description of what happened is that Hope Church had spent seventeen years building and perfecting a leadership model consisting of one experienced minister and a revolving circle of lay leaders. Without changing this leadership model they brought in a young, inexperienced minister, and he soon felt excluded, shut out, ignored, overlooked, and bypassed. The primary reason for this reaction was that he was excluded, shut out, ignored, overlooked, and bypassed.

Hope Church diagnosed the problem as simply the result of bringing in an inexperienced minister. They hoped that by bringing in an experienced pastor the problem would be eliminated. Experience suggests that in these situations the second assistant or associate minister also has a relatively brief tenure. After two such unhappy experiences the congregation and the senior minister, often without any major conscious effort, usually make the necessary changes to accommodate two ministers in the leadership model, and the third person to hold the position of associate pastor has a comparatively happy, productive, and harmonious period of service. This is the origin of the warning: Don't be the first associate, be the third! Frequently when a church establishes the position of associate pastor for the first time, the third minister to fill that position has a far happier and more fruitful tenure than either of the predecessors.

A third factor to consider is that Ken McCall followed the normal and very widely used procedure of seeking someone he was personally acquainted with when he finally placed Don Johnson's name at the top of the list of prospective associates. History is filled with stories of pastors who invited an old acquaintance or a longtime friend to come and serve as the new associate. It was assumed that since they were personally compatible, they would be professionally compatible. Sometimes they were. All too often they found themselves personally compatible at first, but that was soon erased by the fact that they were not professionally compatible; and they separated with strained or broken friendships. The minister who is looking at a stranger as his or her potential associate is more likely to examine the potential professional compatibility much more carefully than the minister who is discussing this proposed relationship with a friend.

Overlapping this is a fourth factor that has been largely overlooked in ministerial placement. An examination of one hundred and forty-three multiple staffs which included two or more ministers suggests that the probability of producing a happy, harmonious, effective ministerial team is greatest when both ministers were middle-born children. Of the staff arrangements where both ministers were firstborn children, four out of five were clearly unhappy, tension-filled, and less than fully productive teams. Between these two extremes were those staff teams in which the senior minister was the firstborn child and the associate was a middle-born child. These were the second best combinations.

During the past two decades the influence of birth order on the adult has received considerable study (see footnote on page 76) but has been almost completely neglected in ministerial placement. Firstborn children tend to grow up to be authority figures and frequently are predominantly task-oriented. The middle-born child has learned since birth how to relate to people different from himself and has practiced these skills daily since early childhood. The relevance of research on birth order to multiple staff teams in the professional ministry has been borne out by studies conducted by this author.

Since both Ken McCall and Don Johnson were the firstborn children in their respective families, the probabilities for a happy team relationship as senior minister–associate minister are not very promising.

Closely related is the fifth factor of leadership style discussed in chapter 2. The best two-pastor teams are composed of one minister who is predominantly task-oriented and one minister who is predominantly person-centered (see pages 42-46). Both Ken and Don are clearly goal-directed, task-oriented ministers, and therefore they would be more likely to compete with each other than to complement each other. This is not surprising, since both are firstborn children.

(While it is both tempting and easy to overemphasize the influence of the birth order factor and to be excessively rigid in applying this concept, it is worth noting that in the 1950s only 28 percent of all children were firstborn. This will mean a comparatively large number of ministers open to team ministry arrangements in the 1980s. In the 1970s, however, approximately 43 percent of all children were the first child born to that mother. What does that say to team ministries in the early years of the twenty-first century?)

A sixth factor, and perhaps one of the two most positive elements in this account, is the procedure suggested by Bill Schroeder. He was very emphatic in his concern that the best associate Hope Church could find would be the minister who turned them down the first time. This would suggest that the minister was not seeking to escape from an unhappy situation. Frequently the most effective associate ministers turn out to be individuals who rejected the possibility the first time it was presented to them.

Another positive factor in this discussion is the issue of need. In view of its history, the sharp decline from the peak years, and the recent increase in participation and attendance, the facts suggest very strongly that Hope Church did need two full-time program staff members. The table below shows the ratio of full-time program staff members (both ordained and lay staff) to the average attendance at Sunday morning worship for mainline Protestant congregations. There is a general tendency for Christian Reformed, American Lutheran, Lutheran Church-Missouri Synod, and Reformed Church in America to have slightly fewer staff members in large congregations than is shown here, while Episcopal and Christian Church (Disciples of Christ) congregations tend to have more than shown in this table.

PROGRAM STAFF RATIOS
(Protestant)

AVERAGE ATTENDANCE	PROGRAM STAFF
200	1
300	2
400	3
500	4
600	5
700	6
800	7
900	8

Finally, there is the question of whether it would be appropriate for Don Johnson to leave St. John's in what was only his third year as the pastor of that congregation. As was pointed out in chapter 1, from the congregation's perspective Don's best years as the pastor of St. John's are on the horizon just ahead of him, and it might be inappropriate for him to leave before completing his sixth or seventh or eighth year at St. John's.

Now what do you think? Should Don Johnson respond affirmatively to this opportunity to be the new associate minister at Hope Church? Or should he remain at St. John's?

13

WHY HAVE A
PASTORAL RELATIONS COMMITTEE?

When the Reverend Don Johnson was considering the call to St. John's Church, he had asked the pulpit committee to discuss a list of twenty items when they inquired about his expectations on compensation. The members of the committee had expected this discussion would focus on salary, housing, car allowance, vacation, pension, and similar items. The first several items on Don's list, however, were not at all what the members of the pulpit committee had expected.[1] The first two were directed at evaluation and review.

1. An agreement that this committee or an appropriate successor group to be named by the church council will meet with the pastor for two hours six months after his arrival at St. John's, to discuss (a) the congregation's expectations of him and his performance and (b) his expectations of St. John's.

2. An agreement that such a review committee will meet with him every six months thereafter.

This review committee had met with Don every six months, and it had been very helpful. The committee brought to Don the suggestions, gripes, expectations, complaints, and compliments of the members; and the twice-a-year meetings provided a healthy place to discuss these in a reasonably depersonalized atmosphere. These meetings gave Don an opportunity to surface and discuss with knowledgeable and representative leaders of

---

[1] For the complete list of the twenty items on Don's list and the agenda of ten items prepared by the pulpit committee, see Schaller, *The Pastor and the People,* pp. 65-71.

the parish his expectations, frustrations, hopes, dreams, fears, doubts, questions, and concerns. These meetings also gave Don a chance to float a few trial balloons to test the reactions to them.

After three years of experience with these twice-a-year review-and-evaluation sessions, Don had no regrets over having initiated the arrangement. He still was not satisfied, however, and for several months he had been pondering a better procedure.

One day as he and his wife were planning a trip to visit her parents in another state, Don asked, "Mary, do you remember that cousin of yours who teaches industrial psychology at the university and does a lot of management consulting?"

"You mean Carl Frederick?" responded Mrs. Johnson.

"That's the fellow," replied Don. "I wonder if he would mind if we stopped by to see him for an hour or two? We go within twenty miles of their house."

"The Fredericks would be delighted to see us, I'm sure," agreed Mary. "I'll call them tonight to make sure they'll be home and that this won't be any imposition. We could stop either on our way out or on our way back, couldn't we?"

Two weeks later as they turned off the interstate highway to pick up the state route that led to the Frederick's house, Mary inquired: "Don, I'm still not sure why you want to see Carl. Why do you want his advice?"

"That's easy," replied her husband. "Do you remember the first time we visited them about ten years ago? Two of Carl's graduate students were there that day, and one of them gave me the best description of Carl I've ever heard. This graduate student, who had been out on several consulting trips with Carl to businesses, hospitals, and industrial plants, said that one day he asked your cousin: 'Dr. Frederick, what role do you see yourself playing on these consulting trips when there are two or three or four of your graduate students tagging along? Do you go out as a professor or as a management consultant or as a Christian?' According to this graduate student your cousin replied with one word, 'Yes.' That's why I want to talk with him. I need the advice of someone who speaks as a committed Christian, as an expert on organizational development, as a student of the process of planned change in a complex organization, and also one who has the ability to see a problem from the perspective of an outside, third party.''

An hour later, while Don and Mary were sitting on the screened-in back porch enjoying some iced tea with Professor and Mrs. Frederick, Don brought up the point of this visit.

''I need some advice, Carl,'' he announced. ''For three years we've had these twice-a-year meetings of a review-and-evaluation committee at St. John's. It's been very helpful, but it's not quite what I need. I would like your suggestions on a better approach.''

''What other models of what you have in mind do you see operating in other congregations?'' inquired Dr. Frederick.

''Let me describe four,'' replied Don. ''I know one church that has a personnel committee that meets about three or four times a year to handle personnel questions and to prepare recommendations on salary increases and other personnel matters. The downtown United Methodist Church has a pastor-parish–relations committee that also acts as the lay personnel committee for that huge congregation. From what the senior minister tells me, it tends to be predominantly an administrative or business committee. In the congregation down the street from St. John's, the elders act as advisers and counsel to the pastor. From what the pastor says, however, that's not what I'm looking for. He refers to his elders as 'The Enforcers' and suggests they are more at home with the law than with the gospel. Another friend of mine serves a church with a huge board of about sixty or eighty members, and he meets once a week with his 'cabinet,' which is composed of five or six key leaders plus the pastor and the associate minister. From what he says this cabinet is primarily concerned with church business, but it also acts as an informal evaluation committee of the professional ministry, as a buffer between the perennial malcontents; and also, at least to some extent, it serves as a support group for the two ministers.''

"If I hear what you're saying," responded Carl, "none of these match the model you're conceptualizing in your mind. You're thinking about a group that is more relational than functional,[2] less church business–oriented and more person-centered, and as interested in you as a person, a husband, and a parent as in you as a clergyman. Is that an accurate assessment of what you're saying?''

"Exactly!" exclaimed Don. "No, not quite exactly that, but almost," he added as a second thought. "What I want is a group that is both-and, not either-or. What I have in my mind, in a vague sort of way, is a committee that will see themselves as a support group for Mary and me as persons and also function as a personnel committee on the type of administrative concerns that should be handled by a personnel committee.''

"One way of describing that is called having your pie and eating it too," interjected Mary Johnson. "Is it fair to ask all that of one committee?''

"I don't know whether it's fair or not," commented Carl Frederick, "but it certainly is possible. In fact, in today's world one part of the definition of a good personnel committee is that the members are sensitive to the needs and potentialities of persons.''

"That's what I'm looking for," declared Don. "Now I have three questions to ask you, Carl. First, what are the characteristics of such a committee; second, how do you select the members; and third, how do I go about getting one created and functioning back at St. John's?''

"That should be a four-point agenda, Don," corrected Mrs. Frederick, who had just returned to the group after quietly

---

[2] For an elaboration of the shift from an emphasis on functional issues to a greater concern with the relational dimensions of life, see Schaller, *Understanding Tomorrow*, pp. 32-45.

slipping out a few minutes earlier. "I clipped this from a sermon preached at University Lutheran Church by Fred Mortensen a few weeks ago. When I read this I immediately thought of an old college friend of mine who married a minister." As she spoke she handed Don the clipping, which read:

> See me.
> Hear me.
> Categorize me.
> Hurt me.
> Play with me.
> But for God's sake, don't touch me.
> > I'm contagious.

The poem was painfully written by someone who ached to be touched, someone who had experienced dull and shallow relationships, someone who felt people were meant for more than throwing themselves emptily about the creation.

"In addition to your three points, you also should be asking how you can encourage that congregation to treat Mary as a person rather than an object," added Mrs. Frederick.

"Now wait a minute," interrupted Mary Johnson. "You haven't heard me say one word of complaint about the way the people at St. John's treat me. When I married Don I knew he was going into the ministry, and I don't have any complaints or regrets."

"You remind me of a friend who is always telling us that we have an excessive number of volunteer martyrs in our society," replied Mrs. Frederick. "I'm not suggesting that you have any problems at St. John's, Mary.

"All I'm saying is that if you folks are encouraging St. John's to set up a committee that will serve as a support group for the pastor, I believe that from the very beginning it should be seen as a support group for *both* the pastor and his wife! Carl can tell you a lot about industrial psychology and how we should be more sensitive to the potentialities of people, but I'm the expert

around this house on a woman's perspective on the world,"
continued Mrs. Frederick with a laugh. "I'm really serious,
however; I have seen too many congregations that take very
good care of their pastor but treat the pastor's wife as a piece of
baggage that he brought along with his library, pocket
communion set, vestments, and that barrel of old sermons when
he moved into the parsonage."

"It's going to be a little hard for two men to disagree with that
speech," said Carl Frederick as he continued the discussion,
"and I do agree that you have at least a four-point agenda. Since
I do not know anything about St. John's, I'll confine my
suggestions to one item on your agenda. You asked, if I heard
correctly, how to go about creating such a committee in your
parish and how to secure support for what I'm sure many people
will regard as a new idea."

"That's one of my questions," replied Don. "I'm listening."

"Whenever we introduce a new idea into a group or whenever
we ask people to support a new way of doing things, there are
three discrete and essential needs to which we must address
ourselves," continued Carl Frederick. "First, people must
understand the new reality. Second, people must accept the new
idea. Third, people must be given the opportunity to commit
themselves to the new."

"That's just what happened at Bethany fifteen years ago in
Don's first pastorate," commented Mrs. Johnson. "First came
the proposal to remodel the chancel. That took a lot of
explanation before people could understand what was being
proposed and why. Next, the committee took about a year to
give people the time to accept the proposed change. Finally, we
had a financial drive, and that, combined with the chance for
volunteers to do a lot of the actual work, was when people
committed themselves to the change. The first Sunday we
worshiped in the remodeled building, it was like two hundred
fathers coming to see their firstborn son for the first time."

"We did have a broad base of ownership of that project,"

recalled Don with a touch of nostalgia in his voice, "and I am anxious to get a broad base of support for this idea."

It may be helpful now to stop and look at what eventually emerged as the pastoral relations committee at St. John's. To do this requires an examination of several different items.

General Purpose

At St. John's the pastoral relations committee was created primarily to serve as a personal support group for the pastor and the pastor's family. It was clearly understood that it was not to be an administrative or business or personnel committee, although eventually it would be concerned with administrative, business, financial, and personnel matters. This sharp distinction was intentionally overemphasized to guide the process of selecting the members. The top priority was in selecting people who think and act in a relational rather than a functional manner.

It was decided in the process of creating this new committee at St. John's that it should focus on relational concerns rather than functional questions for the first year. It was agreed that while it would be desirable for this committee to originate recommendations on the minister's compensation, on the parsonage, and on similar items, it would be unwise to assign the authority and responsibility for these to the new committee until it had (a) had the opportunity to develop and practice its skills on relational types of questions, (b) evolved from a committee into a closely knit group, (c) been institutionalized at St. John's as a regular standing committee rather than being perceived as a "new committee," (d) earned the respect of the committees now responsible for such items as the annual recommendation on the pastor's salary for the coming year or the care of the parsonage. Therefore it was decided that the duties of the pastoral relations committee would be expanded on a year-by-year basis.

Among the other advantages of this approach was that it was consistent with Professor Frederick's point that whenever a new idea is introduced people need time to understand the new reality. By limiting the duties of this new committee and emphasizing the focus on relational concerns, St. John's made it easier for members to understand why this new committee was needed and also provided time for general acceptance before the duties were to be expanded.

Membership

In choosing the members of this new committee at St. John's it was decided that rather than having them elected at an annual congregational meeting they should be appointed by the church council. The basic reason for this was to select certain types of people to serve on this committee.

A special committee had been appointed to bring in recommendations on the purpose, duties, membership, and size of a pastoral relations committee. After six months of deliberation the members of this special committee brought in their recommendations on the membership of such a new committee. First, they recommended that it consist of seven members. Second, they recommended that the members be appointed by the church council. Third, they recommended that, in order to increase the possibility of building up a cohesive group out of the committee, the term should be five years. This was contrary to the practice at St. John's that limited all other officers and committee members to three-year terms. Fourth, in response to the criticism that long terms would mean a new pastor would have to live with his predecessor's committee for at least two or three years, they recommended that the committee be dissolved whenever there was a pastoral vacancy and be reconstituted six months after the arrival of a new pastor *unless the new pastor objected to the existence of such a committee.*

Fifth, they recommended that members of the committee be selected in this sequence:

1. A person who can authentically speak for the pastor's spouse and function as his or her advocate on this committee.
2. A person who can do the same for the pastor.
3. A member from the trustees who can relate concerns about the parsonage back to the trustees.
4. A member of the church council.
5. A member from the finance committee who can relate concerns about the pastor's compensation to the finance committee.
6. A member from the original call committee that nominated the present pastor to be called by St. John's.
7. A person who is clearly and strongly person-centered who can chair the meetings of this group of people.

Finally, this special committee recognized that the turnover on the trustees, finance committee, and church council, combined with people moving out of town, would mean that in the average year two or three new members might join this committee. Therefore they strongly recommended that every year the January meeting of the pastoral relations committee should be an overnight retreat to help the new committee members be assimilated into the group. They added that the retreat should be scheduled so the pastor and his wife could attend for the full period of time.

Duties

The duties or responsibilities of the pastoral relations committee at St. John's evolved over a period of time, and the clearest explanation of what this committee did can be seen by looking at this schedule which had emerged by the time Don

Johnson was in his eighth year and by reading the first few pages of the last two chapters of this book.

After a few years of experience the pastoral relations committee at St. John's concluded that it would be helpful to regularize their operations in at least three respects.

First, this group would meet on a regular schedule ten times a year plus possible special meetings. Second, they decided that each regular meeting would have a major item at the top of that month's agenda that would be the first item on the agenda for that same month every year. By following this procedure they eliminated the expression of paranoia so often expressed in such questions as: Now, why is *that* on the agenda? Who brought that up? What are they trying to pull off here? Third, they concluded that any member of the committee or the pastor could submit additional items for the agenda of any meeting, but these must reach the chairperson of the committee at least five business days in advance of that meeting so they could be included on the agenda, which would be in the mail three days before the meeting.

After a few years of experimentation the annual schedule at St. John's called for these subjects to be the major agenda items for these months every year.

January—An overnight retreat.

February—Listening to the pastor's spouse and children and discussing their concerns with them.

March—The annual review of the pastor's performance compared to the congregation's expectations of the pastor.

April—The annual review of the congregation's performance compared to the pastor's expectations.

May—A review of the condition of the parsonage and any repairs or improvements that might be needed. (This review was carried on from the perspective of the residents, as contrasted with previous annual inspections of the parsonage by the trustees, which had been conducted from a "landlord's perspective.")

June—Open.

July—Open.

August—No meeting.

September—A review of the pastor's compensation for the coming year with a recommendation to the finance committee. This review included salary, pension, car allowance, utilities, vacation, conferences, cost of continuing education, book allowance, and so forth.

October—A meeting with all paid staff members present including Don, the secretary, the part-time organist, the part-time choir director, the custodian, and the part-time financial secretary. Individual discussions also were held repeatedly with each staff member.

November—A general discussion of the pastor's career plans, of his hopes and his needs in the field of continuing education, and of his tenure at St. John's.

December—No meeting.

This schedule covered the major planned activities and duties of the pastoral relations committee at St. John's. In addition, however, as the years passed, the list increased in length and complexity. Among the duties that were added were these:

A reception for the new church secretary when it became necessary to replace the part-time secretary with a full-time person.

Remembering each of the staff members with a card on his or her birthday and a small gift on each annual anniversary of his or her employment at St. John's.

The development of a policy statement, following two

unhappy experiences over the termination of lay staff members, that, if at all possible, no members of St. John's would be employed in a lay position.

A frank, open, and supportive discussion with Don as he suddenly found himself with two attractive opportunities, each of which would require him to resign from St. John's (see chapter 14).

When Don Johnson finally did tender his resignation as the pastor of St. John's, the pastoral relations committee arranged for an exit interview. Several members of the committee were aware that many secular organizations have found it immensely helpful to conduct an exit interview with every employee leaving the organization. The obvious reason is that at the time of departure the person leaving feels a greater degree of freedom to speak candidly about any changes or improvements he or she believes would be constructive. Frequently this interview is conducted by an outside third party in order to facilitate frankness, to depersonalize the interpretation of what is said, and to emphasize the constructive aspects of the departing minister's comments. If an exit interview is to be conducted, experience suggests the process should include (a) an interview with the minister, (b) a separate interview with the minister's spouse, and (c) a joint interview with the minister and spouse together. The report from these exit interviews conducted by an outside third party can be very valuable to the leaders concerned with the selection of a new minister and with the future of this congregation. The pastoral relations committee at St. John's arranged for the minister from a congregation of a different denomination, with its meeting place about one mile from St. John's, to conduct these three exit interviews and to prepare a written summary of what he had heard and to add his interpretation of what this meant for St. John's and also for the next pastor. After reading this, one member of the committee at St. John's exclaimed, "That's the greatest return on a seventy-five-dollar investment this congregation has ever received!''

A week before Don Johnson actually moved out of the parsonage, three members of the committee met with him for about three hours to talk about how his role as the pastor of St. John's had changed during his nine years in general, and especially during the past year or two. Frequently the role of a minister changes between the first and last years in the same pastorate. It is *essential* for the lay leaders to have an up-to-date understanding of the role of the departing minister if they are to talk intelligently about the role of the next minister. Or, to be more precise, it is necessary to define the role of the departing minister in order to *redefine* role expectations as these leaders talk expectations with potential candidates and/or the next minister. (In multiple-staff congregations the replacement of one professional program staff member usually results in a redefinition of role and a new job description for each remaining staff person.)

Another group, consisting of two members of the pastoral relations committee, the church secretary, a trustee, and a member of the church council, met with Don several days before his actual departure to review a list of ''housekeeping'' concerns. This list included (a) inspecting the parsonage to see what repairs, redecorating, or remodeling would be needed; (b) bringing the church records up to date and committing to paper those records which existed only in someone's head; (c) checking to make sure the necessary keys to both the church building and the parsonage would be available for the next minister; (d) reviewing the church property to determine what changes might be needed as a result of possible changes in the program or polite procrastinations from the past.

The pastoral relations committee also accepted the responsibility for creating a special ''Farewell to the Don Johnsons Committee.'' When Don protested what he saw as excessively elaborate plans for the farewell party, Marie Wiley reprimanded him: "Don Johnson! You ought to be ashamed of yourself for what you're trying to do! You should know better since you're a minister. This congregation is involved in a great big grief trip, and you want to make it into a guilt trip by denying the people the chance to express their love for you and Mary and their sorrow over your departure. Call off this party, and the people here at St. John's will be feeling guilty for the next five years that they didn't do right by our pastor when you left. Is that the legacy you want to leave your successor?"

Finally, the pastoral relations committee saw itself as responsible for responding to the grief that was created by the departure of the Johnson family (see pages 55-60 and 195).

As they went home that night, at the end of the farewell party for the Johnsons, one of the members of the pastoral relations committee said to her husband, "I don't know how St. John's was able to function without this kind of committee for nearly twenty-five years!"

14

FOLLOWING THE LONG-TERM PASTORATE

"The reason I asked for this special meeting is that I need your help," explained Pastor Don Johnson as the members of the pastoral relations committee gathered in the combination library and conference room at St. John's. It was approaching nine years since Don had arrived on the scene as the pastor at St. John's Church. "I know we talked about my future here as your minister last fall, as we have every November for each of the past several years. I left that discussion feeling very strongly affirmed and expecting to continue as the pastor at St. John's for several years to come. However, very recently a couple of things have come up, both very unexpectedly from my point of view, that I want to talk over with you folks."

"Oh, oh!" exclaimed Gene Counsel. "It sounds to me as though you're getting ready to announce your resignation. I move we adjourn immediately."

"Relax, Gene," responded Don. "I'm not about to announce my resignation, but that's why we're gathered here tonight. During the past several days I've been approached about two different possibilities. The first was a visit from the search committee at St. Andrew's Church. Dr. Stahl retired there last December 31 after thirty-two years as the pastor of that congregation. This visit came as a complete surprise to me. I knew Dr. Stahl had retired, but I didn't know that their pulpit committee was even considering me until they approached me last Sunday after church. Obviously they couldn't offer me that pastorate, but they did say they wanted to pursue serious discussions with me about the possibility of succeeding Dr. Stahl."

"I wondered who those five strangers were when I saw them get out of their car just as I drove into the parking lot Sunday," commented Elton Powell. "They got out of one car, but then they separated and walked into church several yards apart. It never occurred to me until now that that was a pulpit committee."

"There were five of them," agreed Don. "Three men and two women. They talked with Mary and me for close to an hour, and then this morning one of them called to tell me they were very serious and they wanted to know if I would meet with them again."

"Tell them you'll meet with them," advised Harry Barkley in a matter-of-fact tone of voice. "I know that church. Don, it won't be too many years until you'll be turning fifty. When that happens, places like St. Andrew's won't be open to you. This is the chance of a lifetime. I would hate to see you leave St. John's, but you have to look out for yourself and your family."

"How can you say that?" cried out Margaret Wolfe. "Harry, you sound like you see the ministry as a job rather than as a calling! I want you to pray about this, Don, and I'm going to pray that God calls you to stay here at St. John's."

"What's the other possibility?" inquired Roger Swanson.

"This also is not a solid offer," replied Don, "but I've been asked if I would be interested in a position on the denominational staff. Most of my time would be spent counseling with congregations and with ministers. My hunch is that if I want it, I have an excellent chance of being offered that job, but I'm not sure that's my calling."

"The purpose of this meeting is to discuss these two possibilities with us, is that correct?" asked Harry Barkley.

"No, Harry," quickly responded Margaret Wolfe. "The purpose of this meeting is to talk about three alternatives before our Pastor, not two. The third and most attractive alternative is to continue here as our minister."

What would Don Johnson encounter if he agreed to follow the thirty-two-year pastorate of Dr. Stahl at St. Andrew's? Each situation is unique, and therefore it is impossible to say what would have happened if Don had accepted the call to St. Andrew's. It is possible, however, to generalize about what he probably would have encountered, based on the experiences of other ministers who have followed long-term pastorates.

The Interim Pastorate

One possibility, for example, is that Dr. Stahl had been promising the people at St. Andrew's that he was going to retire when he reached his sixty-fifth birthday. He celebrated that birthday early in his twenty-ninth year at St. Andrew's but did not retire. As the months began to turn into years, some of the leaders expressed their impatience, and finally, under increasing pressure, Dr. Stahl announced that the thirty-second anniversary of his coming to St. Andrew's would be his final Sunday and that the following week he planned to move to Roswell, New Mexico. In a situation such as that, for example, Don probably could come to St. Andrew's and enjoy a long and happy pastorate. For all practical purposes Don would be following a minister who had been his own interim successor. Dr. Stahl would have provided a three-year transitional period between his own twenty-nine-year pastorate and Don's arrival.

Another possibility would be that Don would be following a dynamic, effective, and beloved Dr. Stahl who had retired at age sixty-five to the regret of every member of St. Andrew's. In this situation Don might be the "unintentional" interim pastor and spend much of a fourteen- to thirty-month pastorate (a) dealing with the grief over Dr. Stahl's departure, (b) feeling rebuffed as a trespasser in someone else's pulpit, and (c) wondering why he had ever left St. John's.[1]

---

[1] For a longer discussion of the unintentional interim pastorate, see Schaller, *The Pastor and the People*, pp. 56-64.

A third possibility would be for St. Andrew's to seek an intentional interim pastor to follow Dr. Stahl and to bridge the transition between two "permanent" pastorates. (See chapter 15.) Twelve to twenty months later they could approach Don, and he could look forward to the probability of a happy and effective pastorate at St. Andrew's.

A fourth possibility would be for Don to follow immediately after Dr. Stahl as he is being urged to do by the pulpit search committee of that congregation.

What would he encounter in that set of circumstances? Several of these factors have been described in chapter 2, including the probable consequences of a drop of twenty years or more in the age of the pastor; the shift from a pastor born in one era, who was influenced in his youth and formative years by one value system, to a pastor who spent his formative years in an entirely different era and was molded by a different set of norms; the implications of a possible change from a predominantly person-oriented pastor in Dr. Stahl to the predominantly task-oriented and goal-oriented Don Johnson; perhaps a sharp change in the style of ministerial leadership from the two-handed set shot of Dr. Stahl to the one-handed jump shot of Don Johnson; perhaps the need for Don to change from a shepherd to a rancher; possibly a change in both self-expectations and congregational expectations about the role of the minister's wife; and, almost certainly, the need to respond to the grief felt by many over the departure of Dr. and Mrs. Stahl. In addition, there are four other factors, plus three caution signs for the congregation, that everyone involved would be well advised to be aware of if Don is chosen to follow the thirty-two-year pastorate of Dr. Stahl at St. Andrew's.

Rewriting the Rules

Perhaps the most subtle of the many changes accompanying the termination of a long pastorate and the calling of a new minister is the rewriting of the rules. One of the reasons for this is that most congregations do not believe they even have a set of rules. In every congregation, however, there are rules, customs, traditions, policies, and "the way we have always done it here" concept. Most of these are unwritten, and they are not the same at St. Andrew's as they are at St. John's!

Unfortunately, a common method of helping the new minister become acquainted with the rules is to tell him about them one at a time—and only after he unknowingly has broken that rule or violated that custom.

A better and more creative approach is to recognize that the termination of a long pastorate requires rewriting the rules. The greater the degree of intentionality and the greater the emphasis on ministry goals, on outreach, and on contemporary goals, the more likely that these efforts in rewriting the rules will be a productive process.

Among the most common examples of what it means to rewrite the rules is revising the constitution and/or organizational structure to include more youth and young adults in leadership roles. A structural change to emphasize counting the yes votes rather than the no votes on decisions on program may occur. Expectations of the role of the pastor may change. Intentional efforts may be made to make it easier for newcomers to be assimilated into the fellowship circle of the congregation. Changes in the expectations of the lay leaders of the various boards, departments, and committees may develop. Such changes may revise the community image or identity of this church (see chapter 7).

The Monuments to the Past

Less frequent than rewriting the rules, but far more difficult, is another change that may follow the end of the long pastorate. This involves plans for program and buildings, which often were many years in the making but were not implemented until near the end of that long pastorate and became obsolete with the change of ministers.

One example of this can be seen at Bethel Church, where the minister retired in 1967 at the end of a pastorate that began when he was a twenty-eight-year-old preacher back in 1925. For most of those forty-two years, the Bethel congregation met in a white frame building that forced the congregation, because of lack of space, to have two worship services every Sunday morning. Finally, after many years of planning and fund-raising, construction on a completely new church building at a new site began in late 1963. The same autumn the minister's wife died after a long illness. A few months later, while the new church building was in the early stages of construction, the pastor urged that the plans be altered to include a five-room, one-bedroom parsonage next to the auditorium. The combination of this minister's long tenure and the leaders' sympathy with him in his grief over the loss of his beloved wife prevented the building committee from even revising, much less opposing, the pastor's suggestion. The building was completed in November of 1964. The sixty-seven-year-old minister moved into his convenient parsonage and retired thirty-three months later.

Upon his retirement the congregation found it had on its hands (a) a small, five-room parsonage with only one bedroom and a large and attractively furnished pastor's study that had two entrances—one from the auditorium and one from the parsonage kitchen; and (b) the problem of finding a candidate for the vacant pulpit who would be comfortable in these living quarters. It also found itself with a sanctuary that could seat five hundred, planned in 1952 when the combined attendance at the two worship services averaged 320; but the attendance had dropped to 160 by the time the new building was completed. The number-one expectation of the new minister was that he would be able to fill all those empty pews. The number-two expectation was that he would raise the money to pay off the $317,000 mortgage.

All too often the last years of a long pastorate are spent mortgaging the future in various ways to implement the plans that were made in response to a set of needs that were felt in another era and that are largely irrelevant to both the needs of the people who constitute today's members and the needs of the community in which the church building is located. Too often it is the successor who has to live with, and sometimes help pay for, this monument to the past.

Renegotiating the Contract

Perhaps the most neglected facet of this whole process of following a long pastorate is the renegotiation of the contract (or set of expectations of each other) between the new minister and the congregation.

Typically the congregation calls a new minister and, in that process of calling the new minister, works out or talks through a series of expectations. This often provides a satisfactory arrangement for the first year or two, but these expectations begin to become obsolete as the congregation's memories of "how Dr. Stahl did it" begin to fade away. By the end of the second year of this new pastorate, and usually sometime during that second year, it often is helpful to renegotiate that set of expectations. This requires a serious discussion among the leaders around an agenda that includes contributions from both the lay leadership and the new minister.

His Own Successor?

It often is helpful if the successor to the long-term pastor can conceptualize his own tenure not as one period of time but rather as a series of episodes or chapters or terms (see chapter 1), each one lasting anywhere from one to two or three to four years.

The first of these for the minister following a long pastorate is the interim pastorate, or the transition between the past and the future. This is a critical period in helping the congregation adapt to a new personality, a new leadership style, and a new perspective on ministry. During this period the first priority is to get acquainted and to revise that network of interpersonal relationships which is a part of every congregation but which must be altered when a new minister arrives. The minister gets acquainted with the potential of this congregation and the expectations of the members. The action alternatives begin to be articulated. The people begin to get acquainted with the minister and to understand his leadership style. A few early efforts are undertaken in rewriting the rules. The organizational structure of the congregation is reviewed, and changes are contemplated. Both the benefits and the frictions generated by the transition begin to become visible. Members who were largely inactive begin to be seen more often as they try out the new minister. Typically this transition period lasts from ten to twenty-two months.

During the second term the congregation writes another chapter in its history. This may be developing new programs, defining a new sense of purpose and direction, accepting a new role in relation to other congregations, undertaking a new building program, entering into new areas of outreach into the community, and/or accepting new financial responsibilities.

This second term or chapter usually lasts two to five years and may be followed either by a new contract with the same minister for a third term or by the calling of a new minister.

When the tenure of the successor to the long pastorate is seen as a series of terms or chapters, it often helps both the minister and the congregation understand (1) the dynamics of change, (2) the reasons behind some of these changes, (3) the importance of periodically renegotiating the contract between the minister and the congregation, (4) the importance of retraining lay leaders for new roles as the congregation moves into a new chapter in its history (see chapter 6), (5) the need for building a revised leadership group, (6) the reasons for revising the rules, and (7) the impact of changes in ministerial leadership role and style.

This concept of a series of terms or chapters often enables the successor to the long pastorate to serve for fifteen or twenty or thirty years rather than for only one or two terms.

Pastoral Priorities

Whenever a congregation calls a minister to follow a long pastorate of twenty-five or more years, it almost always calls a minister who has concepts differing from those of his predecessor. They may involve the nature and role of the church and/or the priorities on the minister's time and skills. Obviously the major reason for this is that they are calling a minister who grew up and was trained in a different era.

A common example of this pattern includes these contrasts. The retiring minister emphasized saving souls as the number-one priority of the church, whereas his younger successor emphasizes the personal and spiritual growth of people as the number-one priority. The long-term minister emphasized the role of the pastor as the leader, whereas the younger successor looks around at the abundance of leadership in the congregation and defines his role as one of the leaders and as an enabler. The retiring minister who was an adult during the Great Depression naturally placed a heavy emphasis on finances, real estate, and economic security; whereas his successor, who may not have yet been born during the Great Depression, sees this as an affluent nation honeycombed with injustice, poverty, inequality, and neglected people and thus emphasizes an evangelistic outreach, missions, and social action. The retired minister grew up and served while the Sunday school often was the only expression of Christian education in the church. He is inclined to use Sunday school attendance as the key component of any self-evaluation effort by the congregation. His successor sometimes places a greater emphasis on worship attendance rather than Sunday school attendance in congregational self-evaluation. He is apt to think of Christian education as a seven-day-a-week program rather than as a concentration into one hour on Sunday morning.

The congregation that can understand that when they called a new minister to follow a long pastorate they also called into this church a different set of priorities for both the minister and the congregation will be able to avoid a lot of unnecessary and unproductive conflict.

Caution!

In almost every congregation in which a new minister is called to follow a long pastorate, the observance of three caution signs can greatly increase the possibilities that this will be a happy, productive, and effective pastorate.

Perhaps the universal caution sign is the temptation to call a successor to that long pastorate and then relax: "We've done our job. We had to find an outstanding minister for a tough job. We've completed our assignment; now it's up to him to lead us as we move into a new era in the history of this congregation." Such an attitude ignores the agenda described in the previous pages and greatly increases the chances of this being a short pastorate followed by the calling of another minister. A more productive approach is to recognize that calling a successor is only the first step of the transition into a new era.

A second caution is that often there is an unintentional effort to build failure into the process by expecting the successor to be a carbon copy of the long-term minister rather than assuming that a change of pastors usually means change for the congregation.

A third caution sign is that everyone, including the predecessor, must recognize that the new minister is now the pastor of all the people in that congregation. One of the most widely used methods of unintentionally undercutting the ministry of the person following a long pastorate is for members to turn to some other minister for weddings, funerals, and baptisms. It is of critical importance that the new minister be seen as the pastor and that he receive the complete loyalty of every person. The past is past. Rather than defending or reliving the past, the emphasis must be placed on faithfulness and obedience to the call of the Lord today, not on loyalty to the past or on attempts to perpetuate or re-create yesterday.

15

THE INTENTIONAL INTERIM PASTOR

"Well, I guess we're back to where we were about nine years ago," commented Jack Peterson to Betty White as they greeted each other after worship on Sunday morning at St. John's Church. Jack had chaired the pulpit nominating committee that had brought Don Johnson to St. John's. Betty White had been one of the most thoughtful and hard-working members of that committee. The previous Tuesday evening Don Johnson had submitted his letter of resignation to the church council and advised them that his decision would be announced to the congregation on Sunday. While Jack and Betty both had heard the news on the previous Wednesday, each one of them was still displaying signs of shock, sorrow, and regret over the news that their pastor and friend soon would be leaving.

"No, Jack, I don't believe we're back where we were nine years ago," replied Betty as she and Jack stood to one side and watched the people stream out of the church building and into the parking lot. "First of all, we're a different congregation. My guess is that half of the people here this morning have joined St. John's since Don arrived nine years ago. He's leaving a different group of people than he met when he came in. Second, while I regret very much Don's departure, he is leaving St. John's in far better condition psychologically, spiritually, emotionally, financially, statistically, and in every other way than he found it nine years ago. We were on a downward curve after several years on a plateau when Don came. Now we are on an upward curve again. Third, I think whoever follows Don is going to have a more difficult time than Don had when he came."

"I'll agree with you on all three points," replied Jack

Peterson, ''and especially on your last one. As you recall, while Pastor Case and I were always good friends, I was one of those who advised him that the time had come to move. Those two battles we had over confirmation and music took away a lot of Pastor Case's earlier support. It was a lot easier for someone to follow him than it will be for someone to follow Pastor Johnson!''

What are the chances of the minister who follows Don Johnson at St. John's enjoying an effective pastorate? To some degree that will depend on the successor, his gifts, talents, personality, and commitment. To a substantial degree, however, the nature of the successor's tenure will be influenced by what the people at St. John's do or do not do.

A third factor, which often is overlooked, is what happens between Don's departure and the arrival of his successor. One of the most significant contemporary trends in American Protestantism is intentionally to lengthen that period of time between the departure of one minister and the arrival of the next. The only major exception to this generalization is The United Methodist Church, where (a) the appointive system tends to take better care of the ministers than of the churches and (b) the system of ministerial placement is perceived primarily in functional terms, while in the call-system churches ministerial placement is perceived primarily in relational terms. This second factor can be seen most clearly in the contrasting responses to the grief aroused by the departure of a minister and his family.

As society continues to move in the direction of a greater recognition of the importance of relational concerns, more churches will intentionally turn to the short-term interim pastor to fill that time period between the departure of one minister and the arrival of the next.

Why?

In general terms the basic advantage of an intentional interim pastorate is to give the members the time (a) to do those things, including setting the direction for the future, which often need to be done to clarify expectations of the next pastor, (b) to increase the chances that the next minister will have a long (at least five to eight years) and effective ministry here, (c) to reinforce the concept of the ministry of the laity, (d) to "put our house in order" so the new minister can devote his energies to the present and the future rather than to reliving and being asked to reconstruct the past, (e) to increase the freedom of choice open to the call of pulpit committee in searching for a new minister (frequently congregations seek a new minister who is strong in those areas where the previous minister was perceived as weak; the intentional interim pastorate allows sufficient time to pass to reduce this tendency), and (f) to respond to the grief aroused about the departure of the previous minister and his family.

The major argument against the intentional interim pastorate is that is usually consumes a long period of time, typically fourteen to twenty-two months. This is an especially influential factor to those (a) who want to get on with the business of the church, (b) who see the pastor as *the* leader rather than as one of the leaders in the meeting, (c) who want the next minister to be the opposite of the one about to leave, (d) who are strongly task- or issue-oriented, or (e) who think in functional rather than relational terms.

Responsibilities of the Intentional Interim Pastor

While it must be emphasized very strongly that each situation is different and the role and goals of the intentional interim pastor should be tailored to the unique characterisitics of that congregation, there are several responsibilities that recur with great frequency. It may be helpful to describe eight of these very briefly.

A. Work Through the Grief

Whenever a minister leaves, some members feel a sense of sorrow, regret, and grief. Often it is better to work through this grief with an intentional interim pastor and thus clear the agenda for the new minister.

B. Listen to the Hurts and Ideas

In every large congregation there are many people who feel neglected, who have been hurt (often unintentionally and without anyone's being aware of the hurt), who have ideas and suggestions and who feel they have not been heard. The intentional interim between permanent pastorates provides an opportunity for these people to speak out. This requires a systematic "listening" program by members calling on members.

C. Rebuild the Trust Level

Frequently this interim period also is a good time for rebuilding the level of trust among the members of the congregation. This is especially important when the congregation has been divided over issues or personalities.

D. Define the Basis for Unity

In every human organization people tend to drift in the direction of seeking unity in conformity of thought, word, and deed. The interim is a period devoid of the distraction of "how does the minister feel about that" and thus serves to reemphasize that Christians find their basic unity in Jesus Christ.

E. Rebuild the Base

In every large congregation there is a gap between the size of the membership circle and the size of the fellowship circle. The interim period should be seen as an opportunity to enlarge the size of the fellowship circle and to increase the number of small groups within that fellowship circle.

F. Set the Direction

In many religious congregations the history of that group of people can be divided into chapters that coincide with the coming and going of ministers. Instead of waiting for the new minister to set the direction, it usually is better to have the laity establish the direction and then choose a minister who will be supportive of this decision and possess the skills to help implement that decision.

G. Define Desired Leadership Qualities

Closely related to the above paragraph is the value of an interim pastorate in enabling the leaders to reflect on and to define the most essential leadership qualities to be given a high priority in the search for a new minister.

H. Establish Expectations

The intentional interim also allows the laity to establish their expectations for the future for the congregation and for the priorities on the time and energy of the next minister. Unless these expectations have been articulated in advance of the search for a new minister, it will be very difficult to develop a contract on mutual expectations with the next minister.

This is one means of wiping the slate clean of past expectations, understandings, and misunderstandings and beginning the discussions with the new minister with a clean slate as that new pastor begins a new chapter.

Characteristics of the Intentional Interim Pastor

The intentional interim pastor may be: a retired military chaplain who sees the interim pastorate as a meaningful career for five to ten years before his full retirement from the active ministry; an older regional denominational executive who sees this as a career for which his experience has prepared him for the few years remaining before retirement; the career pastor who spends a few years as an intentional interim before moving to the sun in Florida or Arizona; a minister who has had three or four effective pastorates but who wants a more frequent change of pace; the minister who served as a college president and finishes his ministerial career as an intentional interim; a bishop who chose not to continue in that office but who is too vigorous to go into a passive retirement; or the seminary teacher who chose early retirement in order to spend his final years in the pastorate. Regardless of his previous experience, the most effective interim minister usually is a model of:

1. A committed Christian.
2. A mature and secure person.
3. A person who does not possess personal, ego-centered career ambitions that have to be fulfilled here as an interim pastor.
4. A stabilizing force.
5. A reconciling figure.
6. An effective and active listener who can listen with understanding and grace.
7. A sustainer of morale and trust.
8. A lover of people.
9. One who is patient!
10. A supporter of the identification, recruitment, training, placement, and support of lay leadership.
11. An outsider who has no ties to either the past or future of this congregation.
12. A possessor of understanding and skill in helping people with grief and bereavement.
13. A cheerful person.
14. The owner of an excellent sense of humor.
15. One who absolutely cannot be persuaded to accept a call as the permanent pastor! (To violate this is one of the most effective methods of undercutting the concept of the interim pastorate and of producing an unhappy pastor.)
16. He absolutely will not allow the congregation to develop a dependency relationship to him!

Do you think St. John's should immediately seek a permanent replacement for Don Johnson, or should they seek an intentional interim pastor?